Gift Aid item

702

CW00524204

THE APPEAL OF THE CHAMPIONSHIP

THE APPEAL OF THE CHAMPIONSHIP

SUSSEX IN THE SUMMER OF 1981

JOHN BARCLAY

with a foreword by

David Sheppard

with illustrations by Susanna Kendall

FAIRFIELD BOOKS

Fairfield Books
17 George's Road, Bath BA1 6EY
Tel 01225-335813

Text © John Barclay
Foreword © Rt Rev Lord David Sheppard
Front cover painting © Renira Barclay
Drawings © Susanna Kendall
Photographs © as listed on page 10

First published 2002
This revised edition 2015

ISBN: 978 0 9568511 6 1

Printed and bound in Great Britain by
CPI Antony Rowe, Bumper's Farm, Chippenham, Wilts

to Mary-Lou

CONTENTS

Preface

It might seem unusual to reintroduce a book that was originally drafted as a series of pieces in *The Times* in 2001, 'That Summer'. But I am pleased to do so mainly because it complements Stephen Chalke's latest book *Summer's Crown* which describes with both style and humour the history of the County Championship from its date of origin in 1890 until now. It tells a wonderful story, rich in anecdote and perception, of the last 125 years and paints a colourful picture of society, cricket and their evolution in that time.

This book tells the story of just one year, 1981, and how the County Championship unfolded nearly 35 years ago. It is unashamedly a tale told by someone rather obsessed by cricket and its ultimate stamina test, a sort of distant relation to the Grand National.

Nothing has been added or omitted from the original text. I have just tided it up a bit in parts and dusted off the edges. It's been given a fresh front cover, a watercolour by my wife Renira, which completes a trio of paintings and brings this book into line with my other two, *Life Beyond the Airing Cupboard* and *Lost in the Long Grass*.

That's about it. For those of you who have not seen this book before, I think you will enjoy it and especially perhaps as a junior companion to Stephen's important history, both of course published by Fairfield Books.

John Barclay

February 2015

Acknowledgements

Extracts from this book first appeared in *The Times* newspaper in the summer of 2001, and I would like to thank *The Times* – in particular, Keith Blackmore and Walter Gammie – for all their help and for permission to proceed with this book.

I would also like to thank:

Paul Parker, for first suggesting that I should write something at all and for then introducing me to *The Times*;

Stephen Chalke, for publishing the book and so calmly crafting the end product;

Susanna Kendall, for her wonderful drawings which have added so much to the text;

David Sheppard, for writing such a delightful foreword;

Annabel Jordan, for helping me to redraft the script;

Renira, my wife, for her watercolour painting on the front cover;

and Georgie and Theo, my children, for their encouragement and advice.

John Barclay

Illustrations

The line drawings in this book are by Susanna Kendall.

Susanna trained as an artist at Camberwell School of Art and has illustrated a number of children's and natural history books. She has provided the illustrations for all three books by John Barclay as well as for others published by Fairfield Books.

Her picture of the font at Woodmancote church is with the kind assistance of Christina Bennett, the one of the Eton bumping races with the kind assistance of the Eton College photographic archive.

The photographs on pages 17, 55, 69, 81, 97, 106, 131, 137 and 145 are by Stephen Line, a Sussex-based sports photographer. Prints of these pictures and others of this period are available from Stephen.

Telephone: 01903 243834.   e-mail: steve@squashpics.com

The other photographs reproduced in this book are with the kind permission of Sussex Cricket Museum.

Foreword

by David Sheppard

John Barclay takes us inside the life of the team. That includes tense dressing room moments, when a close finish is being fought; also the wet days that drag, journeys and meals together, and the spirit that sustained a long campaign to make a real bid for the county championship.

Sussex 1981 had a lot of fun, along with that commitment to winning. The characters came alive for me, as I read John's account. It made me laugh out loud more than any book has achieved for years. Here is a captain who believed in his players, listened to them, respected their different gifts and quirks. He knew before the season started that he had a strong team, and he very much wanted to win every match. Yet he was able to stand back, with a wider view of life.

John Barclay is right to say that there was a certain 'Sussex mentality' that gave a shrug of the shoulders, when winning was assumed to be beyond us. I played my first county match in 1947. We had finished bottom of the table the previous year. I learned that many of our opponents said they liked playing against Sussex. We played with a good spirit, believing it was all right to make friends with the opposition. We gradually learned that we could do that – and play with real expectations that we could win.

By 1952, new blood from the post-war years had arrived. Under Jim Langridge's captaincy, we won seven of our last eleven matches that year. We started to believe that we could and should win matches. When I was made captain for 1953, I had high hopes, though I didn't pitch them as high as John Barclay was to do before the 1981 season. He asked me to write this foreword, with perhaps some comparisons with our 1953 season when Sussex had last come near to winning the championship.

At 24 years of age, I was even younger than he was at 27. The post-war generation already included Hubert Doggart, Don Smith, Alan Oakman, Rupert Webb, Robin Marlar and me. In 1953, Jim Parks, Ken Suttle and Ian Thomson became regulars. Ian was wonderfully responsive to suggestions from his captain. I would talk to him every over about possible ways to attack the batsmen – and he would try them all. He had a bit of speed, could control swing, and used change of pace skilfully. He took 100 wickets that season – and went on doing that for Sussex year after year. Ted James also took 100 wickets, with relentlessly accurate swing bowling at medium pace. Jim Wood had great days with left-arm over the wicket, swinging the ball at a lively speed. Then Alan Oakman, until he broke his thumb, and Robin Marlar took well over 100 wickets between them with off-spin.

We caught our catches, sometimes brilliantly, as against Surrey at Guildford. Surrey were in the middle of their long championship run, and beating them lifted our sights to begin to think we might – just might – take their place as champions. Ken Suttle played a bold innings to win that match. At the beginning of the season, I had said I wanted Ken to play in every match. I knew he'd do some rash things but believed that he could take charge of the game at crucial points. He scored six centuries for us that year.

Reading *The Appeal of the Championship*, I realised the major strength Sussex possessed in 1981, compared with our side. We never had a fast bowler who could roll over the tail-enders. Too often, we were held up after we had done the hard work of dismissing the first five or six. Imran Khan and Garth le Roux made a formidable attack. By then cricket was into the age of helmets – and of the greatest influence of overseas players. Sussex's rivals that year, Nottinghamshire, had Richard Hadlee and Clive Rice as their opening bowlers – with pitches to suit them!

Back in 1953, we stood top of the championship table at the end of July. Our batting was strong. Five players scored more than 1000 runs. Our seniors – George Cox and John Langridge, my opening partner – were among them. John had played for Sussex before I was born! He had also played in 1932 and 1933. In both those years Sussex had finished second. He raised the question of the Eastbourne wicket. It had frustrated Sussex's hopes in the 1930s. More than a little shamefacedly, I asked Arthur Gilligan, our chairman, if he thought anything could be done this time. He went across to see the groundsman but could not bring himself to interfere. Arthur had none of the ruthlessness that changed the batsman's wicket I knew at Trent Bridge into the paradise for seam bowlers like Hadlee and Rice.

In the event, we went through a series of drawn matches in August. The championship had just about slipped away. Then we arrived at Eastbourne – without interfering with the wicket – and promptly recaptured the art of winning, defeating Notts and Gloucester. The Eastbourne wicket gave us our first view of Bruce Dooland, who in a sense was the trailblazer for the great overseas cricketers who were to bring fresh skills to English county cricket. All summer we had been hearing about Bruce and 'the flipper', the latest weapon in a leg-spinner's armoury. Everyone said, "You must look out for his flipper. It looks as though it is a short ball but, if you play back, it scuttles through and traps you lbw." I was batting when Bruce came on to bowl. Fourth ball he produced the flipper. I said, "I've heard of that" as I stretched forward. He said, "That's the trouble. Everybody's heard of it now."

Our Eastbourne successes gave us an outside chance, if we could beat Surrey and Lancashire in the last two matches. We were all too cautious against Surrey, and a rather dull game ended in a draw – and with it our hopes of the championship. A fine win against Lancashire meant we were runners-up.

I could feel all those hopes and fears again, as I read John Barclay's lively account of Sussex 1981. Enter into it with him!

David Sheppard

April 2002

Chapter One
The Appeal

It was a quarter to six on Tuesday the 18th of August 1981. At Trent Bridge, Nottingham. A lively midweek crowd watched tensely as the Nottinghamshire number eleven stepped out of the pavilion into the murky light to face two of the world's fastest bowlers. Imran Khan and Garth le Roux.

It was Nottinghamshire versus Sussex. First against second in the county championship table. At 210 for nine the home team were clinging on for dear life. The new batsman's only ambition was to survive 28 deliveries and so come off with a draw.

Mike Bore was not a batsman of any distinction. A capable left-arm bowler, his position at number eleven was well deserved. He walked slowly to the middle, the motor cycle helmet on his head hardly inspiring confidence.

It was the climax of a contest that fully lived up to its billing as the game of the championship. The match had ebbed and flowed. Wickets had tumbled in dramatic bursts, but there were some steady partnerships, too. Each side in turn had won and lost the battle for superiority. And now only Sussex of the two sides could win.

Mike Bore joined Eddie Hemmings at the crease. Their target was survival. The home crowd, partisan in the extreme, watched in complete hush each time the bowler approached the stumps, bursting into cheers with every ball that passed, every streaky run. On the balcony of their dressing room, the rest of the Notts team were under strict instructions not to move.

This was a test of nerves for everybody.

Imran Khan and Garth le Roux. What a combination they made: Imran lithe, dark and disdainful to the point of arrogance; Garth a muscular giant with long blond hair and bristling South African aggression.

The players had already come off once for bad light and, in the darkening gloom of that Tuesday evening, there would not have been a batsman in the world who would have relished his chances against them.

Nottinghamshire were staring defeat in the face, but somehow they survived for a couple of overs.

Then came the moment. Imran, pawing the ground like a bull waiting to attack the matador, started his smooth run-up from the pavilion end. His ten team-mates surrounded the batsman.

Ian Gould behind the stumps. Always talking. "Come on, Fred," he used to shout at Imran. Ian Greig at first slip. In his first full summer for Sussex and proving just as intensely competitive as his older brother Tony. I was at second slip. Trying to shut out the noise of the crowd. Fine-tuning every fielding position.

The dependable hands of Paul Phillipson were to my right. Then Chris Waller, crouching in concentration in the gully.

Paul Parker, short in at cover, was on his toes, supremely alert. At short leg was Gehan Mendis, my prolific opening partner.

The young Colin Wells was near the start of a long career, the seasoned Geoff Arnold near the end of his, and they, too, were anticipating a catch. So was Garth le Roux, never to play Test cricket but here at Trent Bridge enjoying the intensity of county cricket at its best.

What a year 1981 was turning out to be. The year of the Royal Wedding. The year of Ian Botham and Mike Brearley. And my first summer as captain of Sussex. The county had never won the championship but, if we could take this one last wicket, we would be fourteen points clear as we entered the home straight.

*

Imran ran in. Legs pumping and arms rolling, a touch of Michael Holding in his style, he accelerated towards the crease and released the ball at terrifying speed. Bore plainly never saw it, but instinctively he went back towards his stumps. The ball hit him beneath the knee on his back leg with a resounding thud.

The whole of the Sussex team to a man filled their lungs and let out an appeal to shake the leaves off the trees in Hound Lane. All the energy and excitement, the triumphs and upsets, the sheer euphoria of that thrilling summer found voice in that one appeal.

Sussex Champions? We were filled with hope.

The crowd drew in a breath, and all eyes turned upon the hapless umpire, Peter Stevens.

John Barclay

Chapter Two
On the Rocks

The previous winter I spent a very happy few months in Sydney. I was playing for, and captaining, Waverley Cricket Club. It was the start of something new, in all senses. My wife, Mary-Lou, was with me and, in January, our daughter Georgina was born. That seemed to be a good omen. Sydney is one of the world's great cities and one which inspires hope and optimism.

I was planning ahead for the coming season at Sussex. I had been appointed captain in place of the retiring Arnold Long. I was only 27 and it felt quite a responsibility, but I was relishing the challenge. I had been on the staff since I was 18; I knew the club inside out and was thrilled to be given the chance of captaincy.

Like everyone who knows about Sussex county cricket, I was only too aware that we had never won the county championship. We had been runners-up on several occasions, most notably under Ranjitsinhji at the turn of the century and his nephew, Duleepsinhji, in the 1930s. In 1953 David Sheppard led a spirited campaign, but he also just failed to win that most coveted of prizes.

I wanted passionately to put that right and felt that we had the team to do it. As captain, I had to create the right conditions and give free rein to the team's natural ability. That way, I thought, we could consign this unfortunate record to history.

How were we going to achieve this mammoth task, which had eluded all my predecessors? I asked myself that question over and over again during my time in Australia. As I captained Waverley that winter, I began to learn about leadership and especially how to use and shape the players at my disposal.

I had some experience as captain of Sussex when Long handed over the controls for a few matches at the end of the 1980 season, but I didn't feel that I was really captain. Stand-ins struggle to make their mark. Now I had the chance to change that.

We lived in a spacious flat overlooking Coogee Bay where every evening, as part of my winter training, I would swim or surf, of a sort. I also used to climb about on the big rocks overlooking the bay as the sun would start to set, and it was there that I hatched my first plans for the summer. I spent hours turning over in my head the names of the players. With a stone, I carved out possible batting orders and field placings on the rocks, only for my scratches to be washed away by the incoming tide.

The calmness and beauty of the scene were perfect for clear thought. Quite often I would talk to myself about how we would play the coming season, and built up a vision of success. As the waves ebbed and flowed, I dreamt up tactics and strategies that I felt would take us into new territory. We had come fourth in the past two years, but I knew we could do better than that.

If we were to win, we would have to shake off the traditional Sussex mentality – the shrug of the shoulders and 'it's only a game'. Cricket is indeed a wonderful game, there to be enjoyed; you don't need to win at all costs, but winning is fun and brings out the best in the players.

I was very lucky to be asked to captain at the time I was. We were a young side, with plenty of talent, and the past two or three seasons had been full of encouraging signs. We had some star players, notably Imran, Parker, le Roux and Mendis; some seasoned campaigners, Arnold and Waller; and some new blood in the form of Wells, Gould and Booth-Jones.

To be successful I would have to make full use of our established talent and allow those with potential the scope for improvement. So often I had seen in other sides star players who dominated the scene and never allowed their team-mates the chance to show off their capabilities.

I insisted on reducing the number of overseas players on the staff from three to two. We were only allowed to play two at a time, and having three meant the balance of the team would constantly change and become unsettled. It was a waste and placed far too much emphasis on the overseas rather than home-grown players.

The question, then, was, "which two?" We had Imran Khan, Kepler Wessels and Garth le Roux to choose from. All outstanding players and all, arguably, playing at the peak of their careers.

Imran was a magnificent fast swing bowler, a brilliant attacking batsman and a towering presence in any side.

Le Roux, a giant South African from Cape Town, had made his name in Kerry Packer's World Series Cricket. He was an outstanding pace bowler, more than a useful batsman as well as a loyal member of the team.

Wessels, another South African, was an opening batsman who had been by some distance our leading run-scorer in the previous two summers.

It was a difficult choice. But I never had any doubt that my preference was for Imran and le Roux. They were two fast-bowling all-rounders, competitive as they come, and for me that gave us a real edge. Nobody disagreed.

In Arnold Long's place as wicket-keeper, we were lucky to attract Ian Gould from Middlesex. He was enormously talented, more gifted than his record would suggest, and he could bat too. He was also a spark of life, with a fount of knowledge about everyone playing county cricket. It seemed that he knew all their strengths and weaknesses.

I well remember Chris Broad coming to the wicket, opening for Nottinghamshire. "He doesn't fancy spin, skip," Gould announced. "If I were you, I'd bring the spinners straight into the attack." Within the first ten overs Broad, an excellent player of pace, suddenly found himself nervously prodding and poking at the slow bowlers and Sussex gained the upper hand.

Gould's knowledge of the form on the racecourse was equally encyclopaedic, and he introduced the likes of Imran and me to his world of Cockney rhyming slang.

Ian Greig had just finished at Cambridge University and was growing into a fine all-rounder, a good middle order batsman, a seam bowler and a useful fielder. We had the makings of a good team.

On the Coogee Bay rocks I carved out a tentative batting order.

Gehan Mendis and I would open. At the time there was probably no better attacking player of fast bowling than Mendis. A great hooker and cutter of the ball, he would always score runs quickly. I was the plodder, a nudger, a deflector. I felt our different styles would complement each other well.

I wasn't sure about number three. Colin Wells was a very promising, eager young cricketer from Newhaven, and he could also offer some useful seam bowling. Then there was Tim Booth-Jones from Hastings, whose calm temperament and cool assurance under pressure would be great assets.

Paul Parker would bat at number four. He was a fierce competitor and a great reader of the game. He had a mind that raced from one subject to the next and was often at his best when not thinking too hard, playing as nature intended. His most compelling innings came when he was in the thick of things in a run chase, shirt flapping, grass stains on his whites and throwing himself into the crease after a tight single before dusting himself down, ready to resume.

Paul was, without question, the most exciting and versatile all-round fielder in the country. He was like a predator; he crouched low and pounced on his prey with devastating speed. If we used his skills well, his presence would be worth a dozen or more wickets to us. He was another all-rounder.

Imran Khan was simply one of the world's great cricketers, capable of winning matches single-handedly. He had a lethal killer instinct when the moment was right. Without doubt he was our most incisive weapon.

Next would be Greig, Gould and Phillipson. Paul Phillipson and I had started together at Sussex, and he had always been a model of calmness and serenity. He had begun his career as a bowler who could bat a bit, but now was mainly a batsman, becoming very adept in run chases. He was also an excellent catcher with whom I had a competitive rivalry. We both had ambitions to be the country's leading catcher.

My batting order on the rocks was nearing completion, but I hadn't finished yet. Le Roux and Arnold, both capable batsmen, would bat at nine and ten and so perhaps we wouldn't miss Wessels' runs quite as much as I had feared.

That left Chris Waller at number eleven and, with a bit of luck, we would not need to call upon his batting skills too often.

I was equally happy with the bowling. Imran, le Roux, Arnold and Greig would form the basis of the pace and seam attack, with two spinners, Waller and myself.

A dependable campaigner, Waller had the added advantage of bowling at his best on good pitches and the ability to subdue the best batsmen.

Much would rest on the experience of Geoff Arnold, who had joined us from Surrey in 1978 and was still one of the most effective seam bowlers in the country. His advice would be invaluable.

These were the key players whose roles I turned over in my mind as I watched the surfers in Coogee Bay. My plans were taking shape.

*

The players were due to report back for pre-season training and practice at the beginning of April. As part of our preparation the head coach, Stewart Storey, and I had decided to get the squad away from Hove and take them twenty miles west of Brighton to the Avisford Park Hotel, near Arundel, where we would spend a weekend. A 'bonding' exercise, it would be called now. For me it was a 'get together'.

It was a strange thing to do in those days, and raised a few eyebrows. But I did not have to push very hard to persuade the club to go along with it. A weekend was not too long for the players but just long enough for us to consider how we were going to tackle the season ahead and generate the makings of a good team spirit. Everyone was there, except for Imran, who had not yet arrived back in England.

As it happened, it snowed while we were at the hotel so we were not missing any cricket. During that weekend Aldaniti, trained locally by Josh Gifford and ridden by Bob Champion, won perhaps the most emotionally charged of Grand Nationals ever. Gould failed to tip him for us but, despite this, the courage of horse and rider gave us inspiration for our training programme under Geoff Arnold's guidance.

Arnold was just the man for this. He was well respected and did not stand for any nonsense. He masterminded the first training sessions and led us through our exercises all summer. That we had remarkably few injuries was due largely to this fitness and training regime. He was also tactically sound and served as a steadying influence on me and a much needed foil to restrain some of my more outlandish ideas.

At Avisford Park I endeavoured to put into practice much that I had rehearsed on the rocks in Sydney. We held sessions on batting and partnerships, on running between the wickets, the different ways to play pace and spin. We worked out how to balance our seam and spin attack. Field placing was discussed, and responsibilities were allocated for our practice sessions.

When we tired of debate, Arnold led us in some team training, mostly games of football. I have found that many cricketers in their spare time will turn to kicking a football. It is not a game for which I have any special affection, but it appeared to be a necessary part of our programme. Arnold, a dedicated Manchester United fan, loved football, and so did Gould, also known as 'Gunner' for his previous association with Arsenal Football Club.

It so happened that, next to our hotel, was a small primary school, which had a football pitch next to it. This was too much for the players to resist and, before long, a match had been arranged on the school playing field. When it comes to football, county cricketers are strangely competitive, and it didn't take much time before even the mildest of players were scything and hacking down their opponents.

Mercifully, this match was brought to a premature end when an irate school caretaker appeared on the scene. He was very grumpy. "Get off my ground," he shouted at us. It was obvious that he meant business, so the Sussex players had to climb back over the fence to the hotel with tails somewhat between their legs. Most of our football games ended in some minor disaster or other, but none was ever terminated as abruptly as this one.

For all that the weekend was a great success. It got people thinking. We had worked out some strategies and discussed individual roles. We had established some team policies and now, at least, had something to fall back on throughout the season – a peg on which to hang our hat.

"Remember what we said at Avisford," was often shouted out – usually by Parker or Mendis – when the wheels started to wobble, if we had a bad session or our fielding deteriorated. Good preparation is crucial to any organisation if it wants to stay on the rails when the going gets tough.

For me, the pre-season period was a difficult time. How did I keep everyone occupied and happy? How did I make sure everyone had a good opportunity to practise? How did I involve the younger players? There seemed to be endless days, which had to be filled. Net and middle practice began to wear a little thin after a while, and everybody longed for the season to start for real.

There were the practice matches, too, which had to be tolerated. We normally played Hampshire and Kent, games I rarely enjoyed. It seemed unhelpful to me to play a semi-competitive game against a would-be rival. I wanted to try out my new ideas but didn't feel inclined to do so lest I showed my strongest cards before the real matches. Thus, we didn't bother to pressurise a Jesty or a Woolmer but instead just played them quietly into form – a fruitless exercise.

In 1981 we played our first practice match at Southampton. I got out to the very first ball of the day so I suppose at least I didn't give away too many of my secrets.

It was time for the real action to begin.

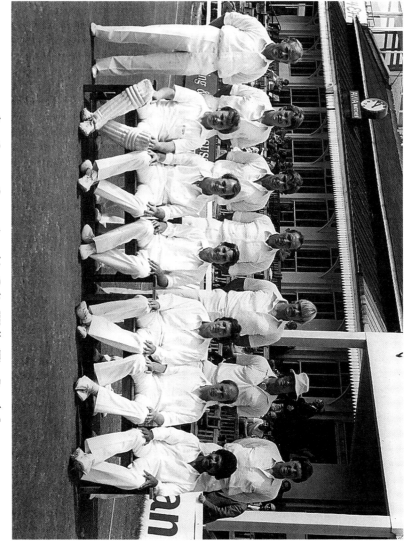

standing: Stewart Storey (coach), Colin Wells, Tim Booth-Jones,
Geoff Arnold, Garth le Roux, Imran Khan, Paul Phillipson
seated: Ian Gould, Ian Greig, John Barclay, Paul Parker, Chris Waller, Gehan Mendis

Chapter Three
Well Bowled, Mr Snow

v Worcestershire: at Worcester, May 6,7,8
v Glamorgan: at Hove, May 13,14,15

At long last the season got under way. On the afternoon of Tuesday the fifth of May we travelled to Worcester to play our first championship match. It was still cold and damp, but there could be no lovelier place to start a campaign, as successive touring teams have discovered over the years. We stayed in the Diglis Hotel, a small country house by the River Severn. That in itself boded well for the season; it was so much more pleasing to stay in a 'proper' hotel.

The Worcester ground is dominated by the cathedral. The river runs alongside, regularly bursting its banks in the winter and depositing silt all over the ground. The floods in the winter of 2000 were, I believe, more dramatic than ever, and the marks, which record the high water levels on the Watergate leading to Cathedral Close, were almost outdone.

On the Wednesday morning I woke early, as usual, and went for a walk by the river. Just downstream from the hotel there is a big weir and pool into which a row of some fifteen fishermen were casting their lines in search of an elusive salmon. It was a bright morning, and the ripples of water were sparkling in the sunshine. It was worth coming to Worcester just for this. I saw two salmon swim through the waterfall, really fit specimens and in the peak of condition. I doubted whether the Sussex players could match them for athleticism and strength.

Then one of the fishermen hooked one. Great excitement. His colleagues wound in their lines, put down their rods and gathered round, shouting words of advice and encouragement. I watched, entranced, as the fish was finally steered towards the net and landed, amidst much delight and noise on the bank. I returned to the Diglis for breakfast, inspired by the river and the fishermen.

Later that morning I tossed up with Glenn Turner. It was his first season in charge, too, so both of us were keen to make a good impression. One thing which Glenn would have forgotten, but which I hadn't, was that he was my very first first-class victim in 1972. I don't remember ever dismissing him again, but I do have vivid memories of his pushing forward to a flighty off-break and being bowled through the gate. Turner's forward defensive was second only to Geoffrey Boycott's. Not a bad scalp for starters.

Turner won the toss and put us in. We struggled through the day, and only an unbroken stand of 99 between le Roux and Arnold saved us from embarrassment.

On the second morning, again before breakfast, I visited the cathedral as well I might after being bowled by Inchmore for nought the day before. There was an early service about to start so I joined a very small gathering and sat down at the back of one of the side chapels. The service was short, but it put me in the right frame of mind for the day and new season ahead.

It has always been a concern of mine that one day I might visit a church for a service, or for quiet contemplation, and there find myself confronted by my opposition captain. I worried not so much that I might be trying to steal an advantage by seeking heavenly guidance, but more that the Almighty could have an awkward dilemma on his hands. Should He try to be fair and reward both captains equally for their faith? As ties are so very rare, perhaps we can assume that adversaries rarely meet each other in church and put God to the test.

The two new captains couldn't have fared more differently with the bat. I had made nought, and before too long Turner was acknowledging his first century of the season. But, just as Ormrod and Turner, the opening Worcester pair, were getting very much on top, it rained hard. By the time the game had reached its third day, the momentum had been lost and not even a series of declarations could breathe life back into the match. We had to settle for three bonus points against Worcestershire's four.

At least we couldn't be accused of peaking too early.

*

Our next match was a one-day Benson and Hedges game against Surrey. Plans had to be laid out carefully because, in this type of cricket, every ball was important; with a positive result inevitable, the atmosphere would always be tense and compelling. The balance of the game could shift so quickly; steady nerves and a big heart were essential. One-day cricket had a distinct flavour of its own and was capable of giving wonderful value to both participants and spectators without necessarily losing the indispensable qualities of the game.

Surrey were always tough opposition. We chose to field first and, on leading the team out, I noticed the familiar sight of umpire Alan Whitehead placing the bails onto the stumps at one end. But I didn't recognise his partner at the other. I turned to Imran, beside me, and asked, "Who's the other umpire?" He looked at me and with a nod of his head answered in his deep voice. "His name is Shakoor Rana, from Pakistan."

"Oh," I said. "Any good?"

Imran looked at me and simply replied, "I think I shall bowl at his end."

As it turned out, Geoff Arnold took the new ball from Shakoor Rana's end, and we saved Imran for later.

Arnold proceeded to bowl outstandingly well for eleven consecutive overs. Shakoor Rana was clearly most impressed; he turned to him halfway through his spell and said, "It is a great honour for me to stand here while John Snow is bowling so well."

I suppose it was an understandable mistake but, hard though Arnold tried, he failed even by the end of his spell to convince Shakoor Rana of his true identity.

"Well bowled, Mr Snow," he said to Arnold when he finally took his sweater.

Imran replaced Arnold and kept up the high standard of bowling. Shakoor Rana appeared to love every minute of it, and even had the pleasure of giving the Surrey captain, Roger Knight, out lbw. After that Surrey never really looked like making enough runs, and we began our one-day programme with a win.

*

Our first visitors to Hove in the county championship were Glamorgan, a team which, for some years, had not been strong and against whom we would expect to win. Having said that, no team that boasted Alan Jones and Javed Miandad in its batting line-up could ever be a pushover. Alan Jones had for years been carrying the responsibility for Glamorgan's batting on his shoulders and, in Miandad, there could scarcely be a more talented batsman anywhere in the world.

We knew Javed well at Sussex. He had started his career in county cricket with us in 1976. Indeed he had helped us to win the Gillette Cup in 1978. By my reckoning he was a little genius with the bat. If he had a flaw – and it was a major one – it was his running between the wickets. Yes, he was very fast and cheeky, on the look-out for runs, but his communications weren't always clear. I found this out early on when we were batting together against Surrey in 1977.

He drove a ball from Pat Pocock firmly towards cover point and shouted loudly, "Yes." I obeyed naturally and set off enthusiastically from the non-striker's end, only to find that Javed had not moved at all. I screeched to a halt, turned as quickly as I could, ran back and threw myself into the crease, just beating a wayward throw in to Pocock.

At the end of the over, after dusting myself down, I greeted Javed in the middle of the pitch.

"Unusual bit of running, that," I said. He looked at me quizzically, shaking his head. "I thought you said yes, but then you didn't run."

"Oh yes," he said. "I am sorry. When I said 'yes' I meant 'yes, I am not coming.'"

I looked at him with an air of resignation and replied, "Javed, thank you. Now I understand."

Alan Jones lived up to his reputation, compiling a defiant century, but Javed scored only a handful of runs in both innings, twice falling lbw, first to Imran and then le Roux. The rest of the Glamorgan batting troubled us little, with the cunning of Arnold taking eight wickets in the match. A win for Sussex, 21 championship points, and already we had established ourselves somewhere near the top of the table.

CHAMPIONSHIP TABLE – 15 MAY

		Played	*Points*
1.	Middlesex	2	28
	Nottinghamshire	2	28
	Somerset	2	28
4.	Warwickshire	2	25
5.	Sussex	2	24

Each county had to play 22 matches.

There were 16 points for a win,
8 points for a tie, and
8 points for the team batting last if scores finished level in a draw.

In addition, after 100 overs of each first innings,
bonus points were awarded as follows:

Batting: 1 for 150 runs, 2 for 200, 3 for 250, 4 for 300.
Bowling: 1 for 3 or 4 wickets, 2 for 5 or 6, 3 for 7 or 8, 4 for 9 or 10.

If a game started with less than 8 hours remaining, a single innings match was played with 12 points for a win and no bonus points.

For the sake of narrative clarity, matches abandoned without a ball being bowled have been included in the figures of those played.

Geoff Arnold

Chapter Four

Abandoned

v Middlesex: at Lord's, May 23,25,26

When we arrived at Lord's to play our second Benson and Hedges match against Middlesex the rain was teeming down, and there did not appear to be the slightest prospect of any play. The atmosphere in the dressing room, as we looked out over the ground and saw all the puddles, was far from sombre. I have found that there are few happier places than a county cricket dressing room on a wet day. Everyone seemed positively skittish.

Of course, there were drawbacks. The likelihood was that we would have to come back the next day to do battle. And how best were we to spend the waiting hours? I made for the Indoor Cricket School with a few of the others where Gordon Jenkins, the school manager, warmly welcomed us. Indoor cricket was not so commonplace in 1981, and so to make use of the facilities was a treat. The great thing about batting indoors was that it made you feel so good. The ball thudded regularly and consistently into the middle of the bat, leaving you with an utterly false perspective of your batting ability. With confidence sky high, we returned to the pavilion for lunch and a free afternoon.

The rain did not ease off during the day, and it was still soaking wet when we reassembled the next morning.

To while away the hours, we would talk about many things but in such conditions the subject of sex rarely lay dormant for long. Cricketers are not inhibited when describing their previous night's exploits and triumphs, usually to a captivated audience. Although an outsider might frown upon such lewd behaviour, I certainly recognised its value. These 'sharing-of-news' sessions were extremely good for the team.

Fantasy was never far off the agenda. That particular morning, with next to no prospect of play, the chief topic of conversation was Lady Diana Spencer. Ever since her engagement to Prince Charles in February, she had scarcely been out of the newspapers. She had captured the imagination of many people including, it seemed, the entire Sussex team, who would drool over her pictures in the papers. It was a necessary preliminary to the day's play.

"What a little darling she is," Gould would keep repeating.

"She's too good for you, Gouldy," Imran would boom from his corner of the dressing room. And, with Imran, nothing was ever said quietly. "More my type."

Paul Parker would read his paper impassively, rarely looking up. But it wouldn't be long before everyone was chipping in with their opinions. The quality of discussion would slide downhill until it became smutty – or worse.

The Lady Diana banter was always good value and kept us going for much of the summer. But, interesting and absorbing though it was, for me sex was something that should happen elsewhere. So I slid quietly out of the big dressing room, walked through the empty Long Room and paddled out onto the field where Mike Brearley, the Middlesex captain, was sloshing about rather grumpily in a pair of Wellington boots.

Middlesex's group match against the Minor Counties had been abandoned, and so they badly needed to play this game to stand a chance of qualifying for the quarter-finals. Brearley, never one to concede defeat easily, was nevertheless hard-pushed to show any optimism as he squelched about tentatively on the sodden turf.

"Pretty hopeless," I ventured in a gloomy tone, although inwardly I was happy enough. An abandoned match would suit us well, since we already had a victory under our belt.

"It should dry quickly," Mike answered, without much conviction.

The umpires Lloyd Budd and Roy Palmer had joined us. "Early lunch," they suggested.

Normally, in waterlogged conditions such as these, the game would be called off without more ado, but at Lord's, headquarters of cricket, the umpires tended to be on their guard and therefore more cautious about reaching a final decision.

I relayed the news to the Sussex team, who by now had quietened down. There was to be an early lunch and, as I saw it, there was absolutely no chance of any play. Paul Parker had noticed in the paper that there was a good concert at the Festival Hall that evening, with music by Mozart, Haydn, Bruch and Mendelssohn.

But Brearley was at his most obdurate during further pitch inspections. I pottered around the cricket square, prodding a number of soggy areas with my shoe and bringing up water.

"It's really not up to much," I called across to Brearley. "It's waterlogged here where the slips would stand."

Brearley looked at me stonily and replied, with just a hint of sarcasm, "I don't think slips will come into play too often in a ten-over slog."

Irritated that I had been outdone in this minor skirmish of words, I tried again. "But it's also where mid-on would stand when the bowling's at the pavilion end." He gave me a resigned look. One-all, I thought.

Actually, I had huge admiration for Brearley. He was undoubtedly a superb captain, imaginative and flexible, and with a wonderful clarity of mind. You also felt that he could turn his mind to anything complex and come up with simple solutions. He made everything seem so clear but, at the same time, never talked down to people.

He was also generous in giving advice, as I had experienced the year before at Hove – during one of my first games standing in as captain. Middlesex were storming their way to the county championship, fronted by the outstanding bowling attack of Daniel, van der Bijl, Selvey, Edmonds and Emburey. I had won the toss on a sunny day and chosen to field. I can't remember quite why but, perhaps instinctively, I wanted to delay batting against such a powerful line-up of bowlers. Middlesex scored 360 for four by the end of the first day, and Brearley himself made 114.

Over a drink that evening, Brearley told me that he thought I had made the wrong decision. But he added by way of encouragement, "You must always remember, and it should be of some comfort to you, that the outcome of your efforts each day are not within your control. All you can do is put in the effort." Brearley took the trouble to make me feel good about a day, which had for me been a tactical disaster. No wonder his skills of handling people are now legendary.

But even Brearley couldn't change the umpires' minds at Lord's and, as expected, the game was abandoned. I went with Parker, Mendis, Phillipson and Booth-Jones to the Festival Hall concert, where the music seemed to share our optimistic mood. Afterwards, we set off in high spirits for the Station Hotel in Slough, ready for our next Benson and Hedges fixture against the Minor Counties.

An abandoned match against Middlesex, who now couldn't qualify for the quarter-finals, suited us well, but it was important that we didn't slip up in our game against a team whom we would be expected to beat easily.

*

Unsurprisingly, the ground at Slough was under water. For the third day in a row, there was little, if any, prospect of play. I think it was Garth le Roux who, after lunch, suggested that he would like to visit my old school, Eton College, which was only a short distance away. This met with popular approval, and several other players decided to come too, Imran, Greig, Phillipson and Gould among them.

Le Roux was the classic tourist. Everywhere he went, his camera went with him. He was absolutely in his element among the beautiful buildings and unusual traditions of Eton. He snapped away happily, capturing anything and anyone on film, completely absorbed by the mysterious ways of the old school.

As the afternoon wore on, enthusiasm for sight-seeing began to wear a bit thin. Our thoughts turned to food, and I knew just the place. The Cockpit, on the High Street, served traditional – and I mean very traditional – English teas. We had tea and toast, scones and cream – and poached eggs.

"What? Flippin' poached eggs!" Gould exclaimed, clearly taken aback by this strange choice of food. Imran was just as stunned. "I don't believe it, I just don't believe it," he kept saying. Le Roux, Greig and Phillipson took it all in their stride and tucked in greedily.

Afterwards, I continued with Garth on his sight-seeing tour. He was keen to take some photographs of Windsor Castle from the bridge over the Thames, which separates Eton from Windsor. From here not only did we get a magnificent view of the Castle but we also became aware of a buzz of rowing activity on the river. It turned out to be the final day of the school 'bumping' races, in which each house competes. A line of boats, each a suitable distance apart, sets off with the aim of catching – or bumping – the one in front. Each

35

boat thus moves up, or down, the ladder. Crowds of people, mostly Eton boys, had turned out to support them from the bank.

Garth and I moved further upstream to get a better view. The crowd was frenzied and noisy and made another excellent subject for Garth's camera. Neither of us knew much about rowing, but we were at least aware that earlier in the year Oxford had won the Boat Race, coxed for the first time by a girl, Sue Brown. Doubtless she, too, featured in the Sussex dressing-room discussions. There were no girls on show today, but there was no shortage of diminutive coxes yelling their heads off amidst the commotion, urging their oarsmen on to great things. Coaches, with megaphones jammed to their faces, bicycled precariously down the tow-path barking out instructions. It revived some happy memories for me while, for Garth, it was simply a perfect taste of England and its eccentric traditions.

The next day, the rain eased off just enough to enable us to beat the Minor Counties in a 23-over match. A place in the quarter-finals was ours.

*

On Saturday morning we were back at Lord's for a three-day championship match, but little had changed. The ground was still waterlogged. Brearley was still in a grump. The umpires were still wary of reaching hasty decisions lest they upset the powers that be. There was not the slightest chance of any play over the weekend and not much hope after that either. We might as well have spared ourselves the journey.

Another diversion was called for. While we drank tea and read the newspapers amongst the unopened cricket cases in the dressing room, I hit upon an idea. "Would anyone like to come fishing?" I asked. Silence. Assuming that no one had heard, I tried again. This time I had a taker. Le Roux, never one to miss out on anything and still with his camera slung over his shoulder, volunteered. "Yes, I'll come. Not much else to do, skip, on a day like this."

With this show of enthusiasm we both gathered up as much wet-weather gear as we could muster, checked with the umpires that play had been called off for the day and set off on our impromptu adventure out into the countryside and away from London.

"Where are we going?" Garth asked once we were in the car.

"Hampshire," I replied. "Some lakes near Farnborough where my father fishes. It's not much more than an hour's drive."

I had first met le Roux in 1978 when we played against each other in South Africa, he for Western Province and I for the Orange Free State. He had already built himself a considerable reputation as a fast bowler and been recruited by Kerry Packer for World Series Cricket in Australia. In our one and only encounter, in the Datsun Shield knockout tournament, the Free State recorded an unexpected and unlikely triumph. I had played, for me, with unprecedented freedom in steering the team to victory. I scored 93 runs that day, and le Roux was still waiting patiently for a repeat performance for Sussex.

Le Roux was good company. We discussed the Datsun Shield match and the forthcoming season and, before too long, we were at our destination. We were greeted by my father who had already caught a good trout, which encouraged us without delay to assemble our rods and lines. Garth had never been fly-fishing before. I tried to explain that casting a line with a rod was an action akin to flicking paint at a wall with a paint brush, but less messy. He was keen to have a go, and it did not take him long to get into his stride and find his rhythm.

It was a good fishing day, cloudy and quite mild. The rain had stopped, and insects were hatching and settling on the water, inviting the fish to come up to the surface. I explained how the artificial feathered fly would deceive the fish into thinking it was the real thing and provide us with sport. For a long time that did not happen, but Garth was patient, his temperament surprisingly well suited to fishing. We were just about to stop for lunch when he had a strong take.

Le Roux hung on, rod bending, while the fish, a good one, rushed about this way and that. But in due course it began to tire and was eventually drawn over the net and safely landed amidst a tangle of line and shouts of triumph. It was his first fish and, at the time, as big a triumph as dismissing Viv Richards, and rather more tense. Carrying it proudly we joined my father for a picnic lunch. The fish, a rainbow trout of two pounds, was obviously the chief talking point as my father dished out some food.

"Have a marmalade sandwich," he said, turning to Garth.

"A what?"

"A marmalade sandwich."

"A marmalade sandwich," Garth repeated. The conversation could have gone on like this for some time. "Well, I've never had one of those before, but I'll certainly give it a go."

"We always have marmalade sandwiches when we're out fishing," my father explained. "They're part of the day."

Garth was highly amused. Just another example of English eccentricity. After lunch we caught two more fish, before returning to London. The following day, when there was still no chance of play, we took the fish up to the kitchen and there Nancy, who did all the cooking at Lord's, prepared them specially for lunch. There was enough to feed both teams.

The sign outside the Grace Gates said it all. "No play today. Match abandoned". There seemed something almost sinister, forlorn, slightly chilling about the word 'abandoned', reminding me of the animals when they are brought into Battersea Dogs Home. No cricket, no points and no progress for either team.

As the summer unfolded, these idle days would return to haunt us.

The dressing-room atmosphere had now changed. The players were bored and restless and in need of some cricket. We drove out of the ground, left Lord's behind us and headed west for Bristol.

Imran Khan and Garth le Roux

Chapter Five

All Square With One To Play

v Gloucestershire: at Bristol, May 27, 28, 29
v Somerset: at Hove, June 3,4,5
v Lancashire: at Hove, June 6,8,9

We weren't the only ones in dire need of a break in the weather. The touring Australians were plotting a damp and dismal course around the south of England. They had begun their tour, as usual, at Arundel Castle where, in a shortened game, Lavinia, Duchess of Norfolk's XI beat them. John Steele, David's younger brother, did the damage. After Arundel, they only managed a handful of overs in Southampton, Taunton and Swansea, leaving the likes of Lillee, Lawson, Alderman and Bright woefully short of bowling practice and batsmen Hughes, Border, Wood and Yallop not much better off. There was less than a week to go before the one-day Prudential Series got under way at Lord's. Sussex and Australia had one thing in common. Both were being punished by nature's fickle laws.

Paul Parker and Gehan Mendis travelled with me to Bristol. We had time on our hands and were in no rush to reach our destination. We took the Chippenham exit off the M4 and wound our way down country lanes to the pretty village of Castle Combe, with its little cottages of honey-coloured stone and its tea and gift shops. In the 1960s the village had become famous as the location for the popular film 'Dr Dolittle'. We had tea – no poached eggs this time – in the only street that passes through the heart of the village, then took a walk down the river, muddied and swollen by recent rains, before continuing our journey to Bristol.

On the morning of the match, I took the precaution of telephoning the ground to ask about the prospects for play. I should have guessed; the ground was drenched. We might as well stay put in the hotel, I was told.

After breakfast I did drive to the ground to see for myself, and there I met David Graveney, the Gloucestershire left-arm spinner. He laid down a challenge, suggesting that, after lunch, the two teams should play a golf match. I readily agreed and drove back to the hotel for my toughest team selection yet of the summer.

After some discussion Greig, Gould and Parker were persuaded to join me to make up the Sussex party. Gloucestershire chose Graveney, Childs, Stovold and Wilkins. We met up at Long Ashton golf club where we decided upon the format of four singles matches. The prospects were not promising. It was still pouring with rain, and puddles were forming on all the greens we could see. The Gloucestershire lads were sporting colourful new umbrellas, the gift of a sensible sponsor. The Sussex team, less well prepared, just got wet and had to make the best of it.

Ian Greig was particularly keen to play against Alan Wilkins. The reason for this was straightforward. In previous matches against Gloucestershire it had not gone unnoticed that Wilkins, as well as being a particularly useful medium-fast left-arm bowler, also had an unusually pretty wife called Dot. Greig hoped she would be joining us for a drink at the end of our round of golf. So he and Alan teed off first.

Ian Gould and Andy Stovold were the next pairing. Third off were Paul Parker and David Graveney. Paul and David could scarcely have differed more in temperament and style. Paul – impetuous, restless, erratic – always had the potential for brilliance up his sleeve; David, by contrast, was measured, calculating, steady, a safe pair of hands. Both were fiercely determined.

And making up the numbers were John Childs and me, without doubt the least accomplished of the eight and thought less likely to cause delays if we brought up the rear.

Childs and I wished the others luck and watched them fumble their way down the first fairway making full use of its width, before our turn to tee off. John, who bowled classic slow left-arm spin with a smooth, elegant action, and I both suffered from the same affliction on the golf course. Neither of us could hit the ball straight. Furthermore, we each had the same fault, a tendency to slice the ball over extra cover. Since John was left-handed and I right, we only met up on the tee and the green. John was one of the most agreeable people playing county cricket, always good natured and courteous and almost apologetic when he beat the outside edge with a perfect spinner. I would have liked to have had a good chat with him as we strolled round eighteen holes, but so erratic were our shots, we barely got a chance.

We did not keep our actual scores, statistics only being of interest to the successful. This was match-play and nip-and-tuck all the way to the last hole at which point we were all-square.

Surprisingly, on the eighteenth, we both hit good drives down the fairway, which was just as well, because in the distance we could see a small gallery of six golfers awaiting our arrival on the last green. Now, in my view, there are only two shots in a round of golf that are of supreme importance: the tee shot at the first in front of all those waiting to tee-off after you, and the approach shot to the final green where, again, there might be a group of interested spectators. The hundred or so shots in between matter less.

John and I both took a lot of trouble. I used my trusty five wood, slugged the ball with all my might and watched it soar gloriously, with just a hint of fade, towards the flag and into the heart of the green. Gould shouted his approval. I nonchalantly replaced a small divot and tried to give the impression that there was nothing unusual about such an accomplished shot. I turned to watch John play his second. Using an iron, he 'thinned it' and the ball skimmed down the soggy fairway like the Dambusters bouncing bomb, fizzed through the green and past the hole. It hit a boulder and finally came to rest in thick grass, thirty yards beyond.

"Bad luck," I shouted but didn't really mean it. "It's in the bag," I thought. With a warm feeling of pride and satisfaction, I strode down the final fairway and onto the green. There I was greeted with the news that everything hinged on the outcome of this hole. Sussex and Gloucestershire had each won one match, with one halved.

The news got better as far as the Sussex team was concerned. John's ball was in a rotten position; little room for any back swing because of the rock, and the ball was deeply embedded in the grass. "I'll have a stab at it anyway," he said with an air of resignation.

The gallery was hushed as he bent uncomfortably over the ball. He lifted the club and jabbed down fiercely into the thicket. The ball jumped out, as if itself surprised, landed on the edge of the green and from there rolled serenely up to the hole, hit the flag and toppled in. Graveney, Stovold and Wilkins roared their approval at this improbable birdie.

The tables had been turned, and I was left with a tricky putt to square the match. I missed it and that was that.

To make matters worse there was no sign of Dot either. So Sussex was both beaten and disappointed. How quickly can triumph turn to disaster. And, for all Kipling's entreaties, how hard it is to 'treat those two impostors just the same'.

Golf was, of course, but a trivial pursuit when compared with our campaigns on the cricket field. Although we stayed in Bristol for three days, none of the Sussex team but me even visited the sodden ground, and the 'No Play Today' sign was never removed.

Two consecutive matches with no cricket and no points. That might be very hard to make up later on.

*

At last, in early June, the clouds lifted, and we had our first taste of summer. Two good wins against Hampshire in the Benson and Hedges and John Player Sunday competitions had lifted us to the top of our group in the former and top of the table in the latter. We could now look forward to a week of county championship cricket at Hove against Somerset and Lancashire.

Somerset had become one of the most popular teams in the country under the captaincy of Brian Rose. Its success was largely brought about by their overseas players Vivian Richards and Joel Garner who, with Ian Botham, gave the team exceptional star quality.

A tinge of green in the pitch prompted Rose, on winning the toss, to field first despite being without Botham who was busy elsewhere, leading England in the Prudential Series against Australia.

Let me now introduce you to one of Sussex's lesser-known cricketers, Tim Booth-Jones. A teacher from Hastings, he joined the staff relatively late in life, aged 27, after becoming something of a legendary run-scorer in league matches for Hastings. A grafter by nature, he would blink owlishly and nervously through his spectacles before taking up an ungainly stance. 'Marty', we used to call him, because of his resemblance to the wild-eyed and goofy comedian, Marty Feldman.

This unpromising appearance belied his courage, which was tested to the full by Garner. But he and Parker dominated proceedings on the opening day. They put on 177 for the third wicket, inspiring the *Daily Telegraph* headline, 'Parker and Booth-Jones thrash Somerset'. But this was not quite the whole story. After Parker was out for a brilliant 108, Tim went into his shell and became so immersed in his own innings that he completely forgot about the batting bonus points. As a result, after 100 overs, Sussex had reached 248 for three, two runs short of the 250 which would have given us three batting bonus points and well short of the 300, which was our target.

"I always hoped no-one would remember that," Tim divulged later in the season. "I kept very quiet about it."

There was another disappointment for Tim, too. He fell on 95, stumped trying to hit the wily off-spinner, Vic Marks, for six. Had he succeeded, that would have given him his one and only first-class century. It was just not meant to be. For all that, we made an impressive score of 360 for six and gave ourselves the chance to set up a victory.

However, we had to contend with the small matter of Somerset's number three batsman. If Shergar, the thoroughbred horse that had just romped home in the Derby by a record ten lengths, was so obviously in a class of its own, much the same could be said in cricketing terms of Viv Richards. The man was physically strong, supremely quick of eye and on his day – which seemed to be most days – capable of destroying any attack in the world. What struck you was the sheer size of the man, his massive presence at the crease. His shirt, buttoned down at the wrists, was worn tightly as if deliberately to display his muscular frame. He chewed gum menacingly and banged the top of his Stuart Surridge Jumbo bat handle – they were all the rage just then – with the palm of his hand as some sort of demonstration of his power.

Richards was an intimidating figure; bowlers knew that he could hit a ball with brutal force if they strayed even minutely. In their fear, they bowled him more bad balls than they did to lesser mortals. What hope had we of containing him?

But we had some fine players of our own, who were not cowed into submission. When the mighty Richards had scored just 13, Imran produced a beauty to have him caught behind. "I save my best bowling for the stars," Imran said.

Somerset struggled on to 270, and my second-innings declaration left them a target of 253 in about 52 overs. This was described by the *Daily Telegraph* as 'generous', which, roughly translated, meant 'he's got it all wrong'. To make a declaration when Richards was playing was sheer guesswork.

It wasn't long before he was making his way in to bat. He announced his arrival at the wicket with three imperious fours and moved quickly to 22.

"Should be home early this evening," Gould murmured to me as we changed between overs.

"Too generous by 'arf," Arnold snarled as he took the ball for a new over. "Will you ever learn?"

I ran back to my position at slip and crouched as Arnold ran in to bowl to the great man. It was a good ball, I thought, just outside the off-stump and lifting. Richards swung his Jumbo through the line and sent the ball speeding past extra cover on its way to the boundary.

Assuming the ball would go for four, Richards set off to run half-heartedly. Greig, meanwhile, chased it with all his might and picked it up just inches short of the rope. Richards now broke out of a trot and began to run with more purpose. Greig hurled the ball back with all the vigour he could muster and Parker, who scented just the chance of deceiving the colossus, intercepted it.

Richards turned at the bowler's end for a fourth run, unaware of the threat posed by Parker, a dangerous man with the ball in his hand. He was halfway to completing this final run before he sensed the mischief. The ball thumped into Gould's gloves like a bullet, and he was run out.

Richards was furious, deprived of another match-winning hundred.

We were jubilant and relieved but, strangely, it might not have helped our cause. "That's taken all the fun out of it," I said, earning some hostile looks from the bowlers. What I meant was that to give ourselves a sporting chance we would have needed Richards to be at the crease for a little longer – not too long, of course – to encourage Somerset to continue the chase. As it was, the batsman played out time, and we had to settle for a draw.

*

In our next game, against Lancashire, everything went to plan. Parker made another brilliant hundred. Our seam attack rattled through Lancashire in their first innings. And, despite a stubborn 75 not out by Radford when they followed on, we won comfortably by an innings. Greig, overcoming some early season inconsistency, suddenly came good, finishing with the remarkable figures of six for 21.

Then against Cambridge University, Greig did even better, picking up twelve more wickets. From that point on he never looked back.

'Sussex can scarcely do wrong at the moment,' Alan Ross wrote in *The Times*. We were joint leaders in the county championship with Nottinghamshire and top of the Sunday League. We were well into June, and yet to lose a match in any competition.

It was our best start to a season in living memory.

CHAMPIONSHIP TABLE – 9 JUNE

		Played	Points
1.	Nottinghamshire	5	54
	Sussex	6	54
3.	Middlesex	6	43
4.	Worcestershire	5	40

Tim Booth-Jones

Chapter Six
Not What Was Fixed

v Kent: at Tunbridge Wells, June 13,15,16

The journey from our tiny house in Henfield to Tunbridge Wells was a beautiful one in mid-June. Rhododendrons, azaleas and greenery in abundance. Unlike so many journeys to cricket matches I drove there with my mind at peace. The team was settled; I didn't need to worry about the batting order or who to make twelfth man. All was well with the world. This weekend was special too, in that we were not involved in a Sunday match. Instead, I would be playing my part in my daughter Georgina's christening service. As I drove to the match, my mind was full of the arrangements – the vicar and his church, godparents and family, a few friends and tea afterwards. For once, my thoughts were not on the cricket ahead.

The Nevill ground at Tunbridge Wells is stunningly beautiful. Banked with purple and pink rhododendrons, 'no ground in England more resembles a tropical greenhouse,' Alan Ross wrote in *The Times*. This year the outfield was lusher and spongier than ever. The pitch would be slow and lifeless, encouraging neither batsmen nor bowlers.

The pavilion is quaint. It has plenty of seats at the front, a spacious dining room upstairs and dressing rooms in the basement at the back of the building. Although not as small as some, this dressing room was somewhat austere and with a cold stone floor with showers at one end, and a loo too, but only one.

It was there three years earlier that I disturbed Tony Pigott just before he made his debut for Sussex as a fast bowler. Unexpectedly I found him frantically and unsuccessfully trying to apply strapping to his injured back about which he had been keeping quiet for fear of missing the match. Sadly and not surprisingly, he broke down during his first over and spent the rest of the game nursing the wound in this gloomy dressing room from which no cricket could be seen.

For some reason, probably based on several years' experience of playing at Tunbridge Wells, I held the theory that it was important, if possible, to field first on this ground. This we did and then proceeded to toil all day. No one worked harder on this unforgiving pitch than Imran, who bowled heroically for 27 overs, which, unusually for him, produced only two wickets. He tried everything – sheer pace, swing, cutters, slower balls, the lot. He bowled round the wicket, too, for some time, a strategy I never quite understood. Puzzled and curious to grasp the tactics, I tackled him on the subject at the end of one over.

"Johnny," he said, "when you know as much about the finer points of fast bowling as I do, then I will ask your advice." I was none the wiser but, from then on, I always left him to get on with it.

Kent batted somewhat unambitiously almost all day before declaring at 250 and giving us a handful of overs to survive before close of play. I hated these nasty batting sessions at the end of a long day in the field but Mendis and I did see it through, even though I failed to score a run.

*

"Do you, in the name of this child, renounce the devil and all his works ... and the sinful desires of the flesh?"

We were standing round the font in little Woodmancote church. I was holding Georgina, but I am ashamed to say that, as this important question was being put, the devil had his hold on me, because the only thing on my mind, my biggest concern, was how on earth I was going to get off the mark the next day.

"I do," I said unconvincingly, as I stared into the undisturbed water at the bottom of the font. The trouble with cricket is that it is all-consuming; it takes you over and lets the devil in with a chance.

*

Let it be said and clearly understood that match-fixing was rife as early as 1981, and long before then as a matter of fact. Not that any money actually changed hands. Nothing so sordid. No, captains would frequently reach a gentlemen's agreement on the last day of a match, which gave both teams a chance of victory – and the spectators something to enjoy. It was match-fixing, but for all the right reasons.

This was certainly the case in this game. Our first four batsmen – myself included, incidentally – had all made fifties, and we had declared with a first innings lead of 51. Kent started well in their second innings and, at lunchtime on the third day, I struck a bargain with Asif Iqbal, their captain. I can't remember the exact details, but it involved Sussex chasing a stiff but just gettable target. In return, I agreed that Chris Waller and I would bowl slowly and invitingly.

That was fine except that, somewhere along the line, our arrangement went astray. Tavaré and Taylor batted on and on through the afternoon. I tried every trick in the book. I even gave the new ball to that most unlikely of bowling partnerships, Parker and Gould, who had handed over the gloves to Mendis. Nothing worked. Asif must have fallen asleep, I think, along with many spectators.

Eventually Kent did declare and left us a target of 220 runs in some 25 overs. It was a tired and disappointed Sussex team that dragged itself from the field after toiling for 112 overs, fully expecting a challenging declaration. Waller and I had bowled 84 overs of gentle spin. It was a dejected group of men that returned to the pavilion and slumped down in our basement dressing room. Nobody spoke much.

"Well tried, everyone," I murmured quietly. "Not to worry. It was a good effort." I did not sound very convincing, and I began to strap on my pads in preparation for some meaningless batting to bring the match to its close. At that point a voice from the shower suddenly piped up. It was Paul Phillipson.

"I think we should go for them," he said. The suggestion livened up the sullen atmosphere.

"You're crazy, mad," muttered Arnold, who had his socks off and was cooling his feet.

"No chance," agreed Gould, our normally chirpy wicket-keeper.

Phillipson persevered. "Why not?" he went on. "We've got nothing to lose. It's only, what, about nine an over. It's just possible." There was a stunned silence while these unpromising statistics began to sink in. "Besides, it will give them one hell of a shock."

Phillipson continued his shower while the rest of us looked around at each other. His mischievous plan began to take hold. It was possible, certainly, but would we be able to pull it off? Nowadays, nine runs an over is never dismissed out of hand, but then it was absolutely unthinkable.

What I think persuaded us was that the suggestion had come from such an unlikely person. Phillipson was such a sensible fellow It was completely out of character for him to propose something so out of the ordinary. If, say, Parker had raised the possibility, we would probably have dismissed the suggestion. But Phillipson's remark from the shower had a real attraction. The seed had been planted and quickly grew.

Everyone was prepared to give it a go, except for Gould and Arnold, but even then Arnold, against his better judgement, was quite attracted by the idea.

Every now and then in a cricket match there comes a moment when the captain has to reach a conclusion and make a decision. This was one of those moments. I sensed that all eyes were turned on me, and remember, there were only ten minutes between the innings, so time was quickly running out for this drastic revision of tactics.

"Right," I said, "we're probably completely deranged but let's give it a go. No half-measures. We've got to throw our hearts into it to have any chance."

"Well, you'd better take your pads off for a start," suggested Greig, looking over in my direction. With some relief I agreed and, at the same time, began to piece together a possible batting line-up.

"Gould and Mendis to open," I began. "You'll have to hurry." The umpires, Dickie Bird and Peter Stevens, were already making their way to the middle. "Then Parker, Khan and Greig, I think, followed by Phillipson and le Roux. Then me. But, if we get down that far, we're probably struggling."

So it was all settled. 220 runs needed from 25 overs.

I said to the team, "If we are going to have a go at chasing this target, we have to be totally committed. We can't be faint-hearted, having a look for ten overs and then deciding at that point." This was definitely not one of my pre-prepared, pre-innings talks. "If we fail we are not to have any misgivings about it, and there will be no recriminations. Agreed?" Everybody did.

All hell was about to be let loose. Nervously we went outside to watch.

Mendis and Gould seemed determined to bring this fantasy into real life. Both hit sixes in Jarvis's first over, and it took Asif no longer than a few balls before he was scattering his close fielders to all corners of the Tunbridge Wells outfield. Gould might have been shaking his head when I had agreed to the run chase, but he certainly took up the challenge. Mendis, of course, would need no second bidding. The 50 came up in less than five overs. The two batsmen were swishing at everything. The Kent players were bemused, but aware of the danger.

Predictably, wickets began to fall. First Gould went, bowled by Jarvis for a thrilling 28, and Parker followed soon afterwards. But we didn't give up. Mendis was playing the innings of his life. Khan, Greig and Phillipson all accompanied him for a while, throwing the bat at anything within reach.

When le Roux was caught in the deep, our sixth wicket to fall, I should have known that the game was up. But, unhinged somewhat by the foolhardy atmosphere, my mind was still in a giddy whirl as I walked out to bat with 68 runs still needed from six overs.

What possessed me, normally such a cautious batsman, to imagine that we could still successfully pursue this elusive score, I don't know. Asif had brought himself on to bowl. Sensing, I think, that my mind was scrambled he bowled his first ball very slowly, a lob, which I thrashed out at wildly and, to my surprise, hit powerfully past mid-off for four.

The next ball was tossed even higher, not unlike one of those described so vividly by Conan Doyle in his short story about 'Spedegue's Dropper'. The ball descended eventually. Inadvisedly, I rushed out at it, took a mighty swipe and missed. There was then a race between the ball, me and Alan Knott, the wicket-keeper, a race that, sadly, Knott and the ball won. I was ignominiously stumped.

It was time to put up the shutters but, with the adrenalin flowing, that can be easier said than done. If we had been sensible, we would have settled for the draw, but we had all become infected by the excitement. It was contagious.

Even Booth-Jones could not bring himself to block and, when he was caught by Asif, the score was 169 for eight and Jarvis had the unusual figures of 11 overs, five for 82.

Asif, sensing he had half a chance, produced his trump card and brought Underwood back into the attack. He began with a maiden over to the sensible and experienced Arnold, who knew what was now required in this self-made crisis. Everything seemed to be under control. The final over arrived with 43 runs still wanted, two wickets to fall and Mendis on strike.

Mendis defended resolutely. He had almost single-handedly inspired this assault and was now winding down, as it were, before the end. Fielders were clustered all around the batsman. Underwood tossed up a couple of fiercely spun deliveries that Mendis dead-batted successfully. Then, with the third last ball of the match, Underwood produced his exocet, a ball of menacing pace, which drilled through Mendis' defence and bowled him.

Waller, our last batsman, strode to the crease with two balls to survive. He was by no means the worst batsman in county cricket, but always our number eleven.

Underwood had his tail up and Kent were now in for the kill. Waller played the first ball he received with impeccable coolness. One ball to go. Surely, he could survive that? Underwood, a very seasoned campaigner, had other ideas. He unleashed another fast ball, this time a yorker, which Waller never saw and his stumps were shattered. The Kent crowd and players erupted. In just under two hours, they had bowled us out.

So we had lost our first match of the season, one which we should have drawn but could just conceivably have won. It seemed that our charitable instinct knew no bounds. In truth, Kent were mightily embarrassed. Alan Ross wrote in *The Times*, 'A more incomprehensible and unjustified result to a match it would be hard to imagine.' If nothing else, it stirred up the hearts of those who love cricket.

But, in the basement behind the pavilion, the mood was not gloomy. We looked at Phillipson who was once again in the shower – he tended to sweat more than most – and laid all the blame on him. "It's all your fault," we said with a smile on our faces.

In truth, no harm had been done, and, indeed, it had been a great gesture and one which did our confidence a power of good. The futile chase added to the sense of fun we were already having. And it gave us a lot to talk about.

Imran, particularly, had relished the challenge, and maybe I earned a little extra respect from him by showing that I was a captain prepared to take a risk. We had lost the battle, but had surprised ourselves in the process. It made us believe that we could, in other situations, do things that might seem impossible.

Arnold, though, sounded a note of caution. "Don't get yourself a reputation for being a pushover, skip," he said. "You can't go down that route all the time; you'll be taken for a ride." Sound advice, I thought – at least when I had had time to digest it.

The hard truth was that we had lost, and so dropped to second in the table, one point behind Nottinghamshire.

CHAMPIONSHIP TABLE – 16 JUNE

		Played	Points
1.	Nottinghamshire	6	62
2.	Sussex	7	61
3.	Surrey	6	58
4.	Hampshire	6	57

Paul Phillipson

Chapter Seven
Does He Bowl Fast?

v Northamptonshire: at Northampton, June 17,18,19
v Essex: at Ilford, June 20,22,23

In 1981, and indeed until recently, the fixture list for county cricket was planned pretty much as one continuous stream of matches. The various fixtures in all the competitions, by their quantity and frequency, turned a romantic and pleasurable notion into an uncomfortable and exhausting chore. It required a rare mixture of talent, humour and stamina to rise above this prickly challenge and craft a game of grace and beauty, as it should be.

There was little time to reflect upon the success of a match won, or discuss the reasons for one lost. No time to savour a victory or learn from defeat. You were off the field, into the shower, dressing, packing your cricket bags and heading off before light had begun to fade.

Driving away from Tunbridge Wells with Parker and Mendis that Tuesday evening, bound for Northampton, uppermost in our minds was not the muddled events of the last two hours but food and where we were going to find some in the course of our journey.

Motorways may have reduced the time county cricketers spend in the car between matches, but the fast-food culture of the service station has become as indigestible as the frantic rush in the fast lane to reach a destination in time for football or snooker on the television at the hotel. It does little for the unwinding process and for fast bowlers, it leads to stiffened muscles and aches and pains. Gould had a word for this – a Julius, as in Caesar. Rhyming slang for seizure.

"I am having a Julius," Gould would say. Imran would say it too, but I don't think he ever knew what it really meant.

Happily, our route from Tunbridge Wells to Northampton took us past one of my favourite haunts, a French bistro in a mews just off Old Brompton Road in Kensington. Some garlic bread and a carafe of red wine took the edge off our hunger and, although we did muse over the day's ridiculous happenings, we were quietly lulled into the delicious atmosphere of France. We had walked off the street into another world that was a million miles away from the spongy turf and chilly dressing room at Tunbridge Wells.

It must have been just after midnight when I finally dozed off in my hotel room in Northampton. The telephone rang. I stretched out a weary arm and answered it. I thought there must be a crisis at home.

"What the hell have you lot been playing at?" boomed a voice. It was the Sussex chairman, Tony Crole-Rees. "Have I woken you up?"

"No," I replied untruthfully.

"Well, tell me what's been going on. Have you all gone mad?"

It was not a good time to be talking to the chairman, or anyone else for that matter. What with my being half-asleep and him well filled with whisky, it was likely that the conversation would get confused. It did. It would have been hard enough to explain our performance to a sober man. In the end I gave up.

"It was a slight misjudgement," I conceded, "but it was fun and I don't think it's done us any harm."

"Well done, my boy," he concluded and put the receiver down. He was on our side really and liked a bit of spirit.

*

The following day was for Sussex a particularly undistinguished one. On winning the toss in the perishing cold, I made an extraordinary decision and elected to field. I can't for the life of me think why. It might have been overcast, and I must have thought that fast bowlers would benefit from this. Tiredness may have been a factor. At the back of my mind, perhaps I was keeping to my preferred strategy of batting last and chasing a target.

I felt it was sometimes the best way to get a result – we always seemed to be up against the clock, what with having to squeeze four innings into three days. Getting a result in a closely contested match usually required some adventurous declarations or, as should have happened in the Kent match, the captains conspiring to set up a close finish.

Possibly I saw the pitch at Northampton as being a good one for batting; one on which we might catch up by scoring quickly in our first innings, declaring early, and then either bowling the opposition out or forcing them to set us a target.

For whatever the reason, Northants batted first.

The match had barely got under way when Arnold called a halt to proceedings by suggesting that the stumps were out of alignment and the creases crooked. So the stumps were uprooted and groundsmen summoned. They duly appeared, not happy, with pieces of string and a wooden frame. Before long they had proved conclusively to everyone that their work had been done correctly in the first place. The stumps were reinserted and Arnold returned to work both grumpy and baffled. It had been an optical illusion.

Geoff Cook, Northampton's captain, and Richard Williams, a carpenter and fly-fisherman of some distinction, both scored hundreds and dominated the day's play. The only respite came for us when Cook, on securing a fourth bonus point at 300, declared and left the Sussex openers, Mendis and me, with a horrible five overs to survive at the end of the day.

As I left the field to prepare for batting I was feeling throaty and dry-mouthed, those ominous tell-tale signs of the onset of a cold.

I took my stance and waited to receive my first ball from Kapil Dev. In India, he was a walking god; that evening he looked grey-faced and stiff in the chill north-easterly wind. I observed a cluster of slips behind me as he marked out his run-up. Cook was crouched perilously close in front of me at short leg.

Cook, the very name had unfortunate associations for me. As I waited for Kapil to turn at his mark, the itchiness in my throat now becoming more of a bother, my mind turned back to when I was five years old and starting out at my first school, St George's in Horsham.

Cook was the name of our head teacher, a large, middle-aged lady with red hair, broken teeth and an exceptionally large shelf of bosom, which ballooned ominously over her young pupils. She wielded tyrannical power, the key instrument of which was a small cricket bat, flat-faced on both sides and used with alarming regularity. She kept it on her large, untidy desk. It was dark green with a scarlet handle, its name painted in red on one side, Jeremiah, and on the other a bull's-eye. Nobody dared misbehave, let alone speak out of turn, for fear of being walloped by Jeremiah.

It was a cruel regime. I dreaded Fridays most of all because that was the day we did sums. Mrs Cook would tap her bat menacingly on the desk, while muttering contemptuously under her breath, as some poor child answered her questions. We were given counting sticks to help us, but they were strictly rationed and, even combined with fingers, were never enough to solve these hideous problems. Woe betide anyone who asked for more.

I never did receive the Jeremiah treatment, but watching her dispense punishment to others was enough to instil fear in me. Kapil Dev – or even Malcolm Marshall or Andy Roberts – could never match such terror.

"Play," called the umpire David Evans, and my mind snapped out of the dream.

Kapil approached the crease and let go a mild away-swinger, which was nothing more than a gentle loosener. I lunged forward. The ball struck the middle of my bat and made a strange muffled sound. To my horror, it flew straight into the hands of Cook at short leg.

Out first ball.

But then an extraordinary thing happened because Cook, instead of throwing the ball up in the air jubilantly, merely tossed it to mid-on as if nothing had happened at all. No appeal, nothing. I was in a state of confusion, my head muddled by the oncoming cold, and I stayed at the crease.

Back at the hotel I retired to bed with Lemsip and honey and wondered, not for the first time, how I would score a run the next day. I slept fitfully and awoke feeling dreadful. I was sorely tempted to withdraw timidly from the day's cricket but resisted it. I decided to struggle on.

I have found that cricketers frequently perform better when under the weather or carrying an injury. I have sharp memories of Zaheer Abbas hobbling his way through two big scores at Eastbourne in 1975 and Gordon Greenidge limping with pained expression on his face while amassing 259 at Southampton in the same year. I've never quite trusted a batsman with a limp or a runner.

The same went for me at Northampton. Perhaps I played more within my limitations than usual and did not expect so much of myself. I found it quite reassuring to cough and splutter and wipe my nose with a handkerchief from time to time. "Isn't he stoical!" I liked to think I could hear people saying. "Not even a cold puts him off." These strange thoughts served to boost my confidence.

It was hardly flamboyant stuff. In all I batted over five hours for my hundred. In truth, it was downright boring. I did declare behind on the first innings, and Northants built on their lead, thanks to a hundred from Allan Lamb. The thick drizzle and poor light put paid to our chances just when Imran and Parker were getting to grips with a target of 303 runs.

In this second innings, feeling much better, I had perished lbw to the first ball I received from Kapil Dev – spared the ignominy of a 'king pair' only by the hand of fate and the chivalry of Cook's captaincy.

The draw meant we slipped to fourth in the championship table behind Surrey, Nottinghamshire and Somerset. Meanwhile at Trent Bridge, another more important contest was unfolding – the first Test match between England and Australia.

*

For three days in Northampton there had been a chill north wind blowing and rain never far away. Overnight, there was a dramatic change in the climate and, as we drove into Valentine's Park in Ilford to play our next match against Essex, we were greeted by warm sunshine, blue sky and fluffy white clouds.

Four days in London's East End might not sound like the perfect way to spend a weekend, but this ground was a most agreeable place to be. Flanked by tall trees on one side, a boating lake well populated with ducks and geese for children to feed, ornamental streams and bowling greens, the park provided the local population with a peaceful and safe haven away from the traffic on the busy A12 trunk road.

I cast my eyes over the ground which was bathed in hazy morning sunshine. There, standing on the side of the pitch, I saw the shape of a familiar figure, none other than our old friend, Shakoor Rana, the umpire. It was a most welcome sight.

Abandoning my kit at the side of the pavilion, I strode confidently out to the pitch to bid him good morning.

"Ah, Mr Barclay, how very good to see you," he said, "but I have some bad news."

"Oh dear, what's happened?" I replied, worried he might be about to tell me he was not, after all, umpiring this match.

"I am sad to say that Gooch is not playing. The Test match, you see. And Fletcher is regrettably injured."

I found it hard to conceal my delight at this news but, before I had time to reply, he continued, "And how is that Mr Snow?"

"Very well," I replied, "and bowling better than ever." This was true in the sense that Geoff Arnold was having a wonderful season.

"I am so pleased," said Rana, "and how is Imran?"

"Very well, too," I said. "He'll be driving here from central London where he lives, not such a bad journey on a Saturday morning."

"It will be good to see him," he said. I thought so, too, knowing Imran's legendary poor time-keeping. There was still no sign of him when Mendis and I went out to open the batting.

Ray East, whom I had always fondly regarded as something of a clown, was Essex's surprise choice as captain to replace Fletcher, and nothing untoward happened in the first 45 minutes. The pitch was parched, ideal for batting on, and Mendis and I coped rather well with the new-ball attack of John Lever and Nobby Phillip.

What happened next was distinctly out of the ordinary. I was facing a new over from Phillip who bowled me a wild full-toss down the leg-side. I wasn't expecting this and waved my bat at it half-heartedly as the ball flew by. Somehow I made good contact and turned to see it flying to my horror in the direction of David Acfield fielding at fine leg. "Disaster," I thought, "he's going to catch it." But then the ball, lifted up by some unlikely Ilford thermal, soared over Acfield and into the pavilion where the Sussex team was sitting. They cheered uncontrollably, as well they might for, eleven years after my debut, I had hit my first ever six in first-class cricket.

In the next over, as if to show that this triumph was not really meant to be, I pushed forward to an in-swinger from Lever and was given out lbw by Shakoor Rana who raised his finger slowly and sympathetically as if to say, "I know you are captain and that we had a nice chat this morning, but sadly you're out." 24 runs may not look that impressive in the scorebook, but for me it was a memorable innings.

By then, Imran had arrived. "Terrible traffic in London," he said, "and I think I took the wrong road." How he ever finds his way around Lahore and Karachi, I cannot imagine.

Much of the day was dominated by a fine partnership between Mendis and Parker, both of whom scored hundreds. On the boundary red necks, legs and torsos, exposed to the sun for the first time in the year, heralded the welcome arrival and fragrance of sun cream.

There is some consolation in failure. By mid-afternoon I was licking a delicious ice cream beneath the tall trees with Tim Booth-Jones, whose innings had also been brief. It was while we were happily diverted that Parker struck Acfield for an enormous six that flew over our heads and out of the ground, narrowly missing a number 129 bus passing by. This partnership, which was punctuated by regular loudspeaker announcements of England's latest dismissals at Trent Bridge, was finally broken just before tea when Mendis was run out, the decision flamboyantly given by Shakoor Rana's partner, Dickie Bird.

As it turned out, Imran need not have hurried across from Chelsea after all. "Johnny, you worry too much about me," he told me. "I've never let you down ... yet."

Imran was always well prepared for batting. He would pad up, ready for action as soon as the Sussex innings began in anticipation of imminent disaster. He liked to have lots of balls thrown at him before he went out to bat, as if he needed reassurance of his ability and an injection of confidence. He presented an image of imperious calm but, in truth, got very nervous. He would sit restlessly waiting his turn, muttering to himself from time to time, "Please God, give me twenty runs and then I'll make a hundred." Here, at Ilford, he had been padded up and ready for action for four hours, so he was in quite a state when his moment finally came.

Not that anyone would have noticed his nerves. Floppy hat perched on his head, he batted in the carefree style of the old-fashioned amateur. He announced his arrival at the crease and released the tension in his limbs by carting Acfield for a huge six which almost landed in the boating lake, the first of five he hit that afternoon. The last of these was swept straight into the public lavatories, scattering those who had much to drink and were waiting their turn. Imran was two short of a well-deserved, whirlwind hundred by close of play.

Sussex had completed its best day's batting for years, 436 for four, and all in glorious sunshine.

*

The next day – midsummer's day – we played Essex in the Sunday League on the same ground. The Sunday match at Ilford had long since become a special day out for East London cricket fans who flocked in their thousands to Valentine's Park, filling the ground to capacity. It was a happy spectacle of picnics, impromptu games of cricket and beer drinkers. Bare torsos and tattoos were the order of the day. This instant style of afternoon cricket, with a result at the end, was what the public really wanted to see and enjoy, entertainment which the world over has scarcely reduced in popularity since it was first conceived.

It was an important match for both teams. Sussex and Essex were first and third in the table respectively. With a large holiday crowd milling about, it was not easy for the players to practise before the match without interrupting the mini-matches all around them. I didn't bother to try and instead joined Keith Fletcher, now restored to fitness, on the pitch to toss up. He won and decided to bat. On hearing this news, the Sussex bowlers, needing to warm up and loosen their limbs, looked for some spare outfield on which they could prepare for the onslaught. I went in search of a cup of tea.

I was just returning from the small dining-room in the pavilion when I heard a loud and agonised cry of pain from the field. I looked out to see Imran lying prostrate on the grass, clutching his right ankle. "Ice," somebody shouted. I gulped down the rest of my tea and went to find some ice cubes and a towel, knowing full well that they were unlikely to provide a miraculous cure. That Imran had turned his ankle over and would not be able to take his place in the Sussex team was obvious, even to the most optimistic medical mind.

"Oh God, I think I have broken my ankle," Imran groaned as he was hoisted back to the dressing room for treatment on his rapidly swelling foot.

My immediate problem was to sort out a replacement for him. We had already tossed up and so the teams had been officially declared. I knew I would have to discuss the matter with Fletcher. Feeling rather foolish, I knocked on the Essex dressing-room door. "Get out," shouted a voice, Lever's I think. Despite this minor setback I bravely put my head round the door. They all knew what had happened, of course, and East was celebrating by acting the goat.

"Excuse me," I began. "Sorry to be a bore, but something dreadfully inconvenient has happened. Imran has hurt his ankle."

"Oh dear," came the Essex reply which couldn't disguise its joy.

I soldiered on. "Would it be possible for someone else to play instead?"

"Does he bowl fast?" asked Fletcher, ever mindful of the needs of his team.

"No," I said. "In fact he can't bowl at all. He's a batsman, a blocker, a bit like me, the sort that most bowlers dream about on Sundays. He's called Booth-Jones."

In fact, the Essex team had come across him the previous day, but I doubted his two runs had made much of an impression on them.

The Essex team were quite enjoying the banter and, such was their relief at not having to face Imran, they were quite happy to accept a hyphenated blocker as a replacement. "Now piss off," Lever shouted so I was sent on my way without more ado.

I broke the news to Booth-Jones gently; his Sunday had now been completely ruined by Imran's misfortune. The poor chap, who suffered terribly from migraines, suddenly found another one coming on.

The match duly took its course and with two overs to go and Sussex needing 11 to win, Booth-Jones walked out to bat at number nine. He was feeling sick. He hunched his shoulders, blinked through his spectacles, tried to ignore his headache and swished purposefully but to no avail at fresh air. He was not assisting the Sussex cause.

Eight runs were still needed from the final over. Acfield was called up to bowl. I was facing and, although none too confident myself, instinct told me that victory in this match lay in my hands. I decided to take a chance against Acfield – at least he was a slow(ish) bowler – and pre-determined that I would hit his first ball through the off-side and the next, by way of variety, through the leg. Astonishingly, the plan worked perfectly. Two fours, and it was all over.

Booth-Jones, the strain and stress of the occasion oozing out of him, returned with me to the pavilion triumphant – one not out – and celebrated with the rest of us. We were now four points clear at the top of the table while ahead of us lay the prospect of bowling out Essex twice in the championship without Imran.

Meanwhile at Trent Bridge, on the first Sunday of Test cricket in England, Australia had bowled out England for 125 in its second innings – with Lillee and Alderman taking all ten wickets between them. Australia then stumbled uncertainly to a four-wicket victory.

*

Monday was a hot day. We were tired after the excitement of the Sunday League win, and the ground looked slightly the worse for wear, with the chairs dishevelled and litter from the day before scattered about like confetti blown in the wind.

We did some team stretching as usual and then I walked around the boundary, turning over in my mind how we might bowl Essex out twice. Imran, who had twisted his ankle, would definitely be 'off games' for a while.

I was busy considering our options when I noticed by the scoreboard at the furthest corner of the ground an enormous heavy roller. It was not the usual motorised sort but an old-fashioned hand-pulled roller that did not look as if it had been used for years. "Just what we need," I thought. Sussex, never a team to have made much use of spin in the past, would tackle Essex with the flight and guile of their slow bowlers – in other words, Waller and me.

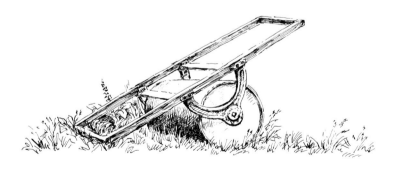

Excited by my discovery, I then persuaded the groundsman and a team of volunteers to drag this colossal roller up and down the dry and disintegrating pitch, watched by a bemused Dickie Bird and Shakoor Rana.

Whether it seriously damaged and further broke up the dry soil is anyone's guess, but it was good to see this museum piece of equipment in action again after, I suspect, many years of idleness. There was a time when the roller was something of a trademark on each ground. The United Services ground at Portsmouth had the heaviest 'crusher' of all, and I seem to remember that Worcester once had a worthy specimen, too. Now rollers are more standard and less interesting. They may even be more efficient and less often do they roll the ball into the pitch or break down, causing a delay to play or leaving a pool of oil on a length.

At Hove, there used to be a giant hand-roller too, which in April the junior players would heave diagonally over the square as a punishing form of pre-season training designed to strengthen back muscles. It was thought to be the reason behind the pace and bounce extracted from Hove's green pitches. Grounds could be identified by their rollers, and here in Ilford I felt I had brought back to life, for a few minutes, an old friend from years gone by.

To have my way with the roller, Sussex had first to bat on for at least one more ball before declaring, a rather pointless exercise in truth, but so be it. Imran spent the day sitting in the shade with his injured foot resting on a chair. "See what you can do without me. Good luck," he said with a smile on his face.

We began well. Le Roux took two early wickets but, with the pitch now dusty and dry, it was not long before Waller and I were bowling our spinners. The pitch was already beginning to play some tricks. Lever, the Essex opening bowler, had dug a most helpful hole outside the off-stump with his follow-through, which I was trying to exploit. Essex collapsed to 80 for six.

Then followed an annoying partnership between Turner and East. I was in the middle of a determined spell of bowling during that hot afternoon when Shakoor Rana suddenly and unexpectedly stopped me and proclaimed quite fiercely, "Mr Barclay, you are running down the pitch when you bowl."

"Oh dear," I said innocently. "I am so sorry, can't I do that?"

"Certainly not," he said, "I must tell Mr Dickie at once." He strode over to Dickie Bird, who was following events from square

66

leg. Both umpires then bent over the pitch and scrutinised the marks made by my follow-through.

"Come on now, captain, you must run off the pitch as you've been told," Dickie said in support of his partner.

The game, which had temporarily been brought to a halt by this crisis, now resumed. At the end of the same over, Rana came over and handed me my floppy hat. I thought he was going to admonish me again, but instead he said such a charming thing. "Mr Barclay, I know you are running on the wicket but, as you are captain, I will not worry too much about it." Surely nothing could have exemplified the spirit of the game better. Essex's innings subsided, and they were all out for 169.

"I'm sorry to interrupt again," I said as I put my head around the door of the Essex dressing room, "but I wondered if ..." I never got any further because very loudly and in unison they told me to piss off – again. There was a certain directness about the Essex team, which left you in no doubt where you stood. Despite not having received my message about the follow-on, their opening batsmen obediently followed us back onto the field for the second innings.

The pitch by now was more treacherous. The batsmen chanced their arm and Alan Lilley, in particular, played a most daring innings during which he struck Phillipson, fielding close at short leg, a severe blow in the groin. He was carried off in agony and Stewart Storey, our coach, in the absence of any more substitutes, came onto the field.

Waller and I toiled away. There was lots of excitement around the bat, many shouts of "catch it", stifled appeals and real appeals, almost all of which were turned down.

While all this was going on I was reminded of a story which a taxi-driver had told me in India in 1970, when I was on tour there with the English Schools Cricket Association. We were not the first team abroad to be having trouble persuading the Indian umpires to lift their fingers in response to our appeals, whereas our opponents, by comparison, were doing rather well in that department.

"Ah, that's easy," said the taxi-driver when I explained the problem. "What you must shout loudly instead of 'howzat' is 'where's Allah', whereupon the umpire will point his finger to the sky and say 'up there'."

Worth a try in Ilford, I thought. So the next time I hit the batsman on the pad I appealed loudly. "Where's Allah?"

"Not out," came the response from Rana and, as I walked back past him, he whispered, "Not that silly trick again."

However, wickets did fall at regular intervals, and we might even have won the match within two days – but for some strange fielding by le Roux, who had been quietly grazing in the outfield, his bowling not being required on this dry pitch.

Shortly before close of play Phillip, Essex's West Indian player, hoiked a ball high into the air to where Storey was poised to take the catch on the boundary. Le Roux, probably in need of something to do, got it into his head that it was his catch. He charged like a demented rhinoceros, careered across Storey's line of vision, snatched at the ball and dropped it.

Essex held out for a little longer on the third morning but, by lunchtime, it was all over. Waller and I took thirteen wickets between us and we won the match by an innings and 21 runs, adding another 24 points to our championship total.

It was midsummer. Sussex, for the first time in its history, were leading the way in both the county championship and Sunday League.

My thoughts went back to Coogee Bay in Sydney and my scratched plans on the rocks. I started to believe that my dreams really could come true. If only Imran hadn't injured his ankle.

CHAMPIONSHIP TABLE – 23 JUNE

		Played	Points
1.	Sussex	9	88
2.	Surrey	7	80
3.	Nottinghamshire	8	73
4.	Somerset	7	68

Imran Khan

Chapter Eight
A Hero in Colombo

v Gloucestershire: at Hove, July 4,6,7

Next we played our return match against Gloucestershire whom, thus far, we had met only on the golf course. We were greeted by a sea fret at Hove, which enshrouded the ground, dampened spirits and delayed the start for an hour.

Moisture in the air has a reputation for making the ball swing or nip about off the seam. Despite this, on winning the toss, unhesitatingly I decided to bat first. "Always bat first on Saturdays at Hove," Parker had frequently told me. I had certainly come a cropper on several occasions in the past by ignoring this advice.

In any case Imran was still injured and le Roux now crocked as well. Bear in mind, too, that we were up against the magical skills of the studious-looking Zaheer Abbas who, at the time, was averaging 128 and had already scored six centuries from just nine innings.

The pitch was not typical of Hove. It had been used before and was both closely cropped and dusty in patches. So our plan was to bat first, just as we did at Ilford, make a big score and then bowl out the opposition twice on a crumbling wicket. It was not a strategy often used at Hove and one with a doubtful track record of success in Sussex's history.

On the first day, things went pretty much to plan. Mendis and I put on a hundred for the first wicket, and this was followed by a useful partnership from Booth-Jones and Parker. Booth-Jones, now just about recovered from Ilford, was always worth watching because of the unexpected nature of his cricket.

He played a ball down to fine leg and set off quickly hoping for two runs. In his enthusiasm he collided with Parker in the middle of the pitch and was completely flattened. His kit was strewn all over the place – helmet, spectacles and bat. Instead of getting up straight away, he crawled around looking for his glasses before, amidst the mess, someone trod on them. Disconcerted, he then made for the same end as Parker and arrived there at the same time. By some miracle the throw from fine leg was a wild one and completely cleared the wicket-keeper before running away towards mid-off. But, by this stage, the batsmen became confused and could not work out who had to run where in order to register either a single or two runs. Miraculously, both avoided being run out and left it to the umpire, Lloyd Budd, to sort out how many runs had in fact been scored.

While this tomfoolery was being played out, the Sussex team in the viewing room was dividing its attention between the shenanigans on the field and the men's singles final at Wimbledon.

John McEnroe and Bjorn Borg were immersed in one of the great Centre Court battles. Now and then Parker, from the crease, would shout at us, "Watch the cricket", but this was difficult for us when confronted with the magical stroke play and on-court drama provided by the two tennis players. Half the Sussex players thought McEnroe should be banned for his outrageous behaviour and language whilst the other half loved it. In the end McEnroe won the match, but was fined almost a third of his £27,000 winnings for his conduct. We were bowled out for 304.

Whatever the conditions or state of the pitch, it seemed likely that in reply Zaheer would score another hundred, and so he did. Indeed I was actually bowling when he came in to bat and, having just taken the previous two wickets, was feeling justifiably confident. Not wishing Zaheer to sense that he had the upper hand from the beginning, I bravely posted some close fielders in an attempt to unnerve him. His response was to cut and drive his first three balls sweetly to the boundary.

He never looked back and continued to dominate proceedings throughout an unremittingly hot second afternoon. No ball I bowled ever seemed to hit the right length. Drop it slightly short, and Zaheer would lean back and carve it away deftly on either side of the wicket; overpitch, and he would drive almost lazily into the gaps. With his wristy style he made batting look both easy and pleasurable. The same could not be said of his team-mates who, in stark contrast, pushed and poked nervously at the spinning ball.

I persevered with spin despite the onslaught. Booth-Jones, who had been standing courageously at short-leg from the outset, was just beginning to flinch a little whenever Zaheer swept. I bowled another well-flighted off-break, which was heaved powerfully through mid-wicket, whistling past Booth-Jones' shoulder on its way.

"Tim," I said, "just come a yard to your left." He hesitated for a moment, blinking at me nervously through his glasses from beneath his helmet. As a relatively junior player, he decided it would be best to do as his captain asked.

I bowled another ball. This time it was pulled vigorously to square leg, just missing Tim's knees in the process. I was just halfway through my over when I noticed that my battle-weary fielder was walking over in my direction.

"What's the problem?" I said somewhat impatiently and anxious to continue the over.

"Zaheer is," he replied. "I'm not sure how to put this, but he's just told me that if I continue to field so close he intends to hit the ball straight at me and hard. I believe he means it, too. I'm not happy. I've nearly had enough."

It was quite clear that Zaheer's intimidating batting and language was undermining my fielder's confidence. For all that, I was cruelly unsympathetic.

"What a lot of nonsense," I replied. "He's only trying to put you off. We'll get him in a moment if we persevere." It was hard to sound convincing, and Tim sloped off back to his position, looking miserable and resigned to his fate.

Gould, observing all this with interest from behind the stumps, whispered out of the corner of his mouth some advice to Booth-Jones. "Ignore the captain. Do as Zaheer says while he's in this menacing mood."

Wrestling with this conflicting advice, Booth-Jones stayed where he was. The very next ball, true to his word, Zaheer swung powerfully and accurately, catching Tim a sickening crack full on his helmet. As we gathered round the stricken casualty and helped him to recover, Gould took me to one side and had a quiet word.

"Skip," he said, "I think the time has come to swallow your pride and dispense with your close catcher." Looking at the poor man lying dazed on the ground and Zaheer rapidly approaching his hundred, I could not find it in my heart to disagree.

Zaheer was finally out for 145 out of a total of 285, the next highest score being 27. The pitch was taking spin, but how hard it would be to judge a second innings declaration in such circumstances. Zaheer, like Viv Richards, was capable of upsetting the best laid plans. So we took a chance and simply gambled that somehow or other we would get Zaheer out a second time for fewer runs. We were at the top of the table with little to lose and had certainly not lost our Tunbridge Wells spirit.

Mendis and Parker shared in a dashing partnership of 96 before I declared and set Gloucestershire a simple target of 217 runs in about 60 overs. There was plenty of time for either side to win. But it all rather depended upon Zaheer.

After the fall of two early wickets, there was an air of expectation and tension as he walked out to bat. Nobody in the small crowd was leaving early. Confronted by the spin of Waller and Barclay, he was quickly into his stride and guiding the ball skilfully into gaps. The score reached 79 for two, with the last over before tea to be bowled by Waller.

I was standing at slip and Gould was of course behind the stumps. Otherwise the fielders were well scattered.

With one ball of the over to go, all was quiet. Waller tossed up a well-flighted delivery around the leg-stump which Zaheer shaped to flick casually through mid-wicket but failed to allow for just the merest hint of spin. Instead of the ball gliding away serenely for more runs, it ballooned high up into the air where it dwindled into a mere speck against the blue sky.

The ball was clearly going to descend in the mid-on region, and who should be fielding there, alas, but the pale and hapless Booth-Jones? The whole match appeared to depend on the outcome of this one ball. It was a devilish, swirling catch, caught briefly in the atmosphere where the wind could play all sorts of tricks.

The ball hung up there in space for what seemed like an age before plunging downwards. Pirouetting giddily, Tim tried to establish a stable position for catching. So long was the ball in the air that Gould had time to turn to me at slip, fold his arms and say, "No chance, skip." I'm ashamed to say I had to agree and, as we watched Tim revolving ungracefully beneath the ball, we had more or less given it up.

Then the moment of truth finally arrived. The ball dropped just behind our heroic fielder; he stretched his hands back and clasped it as he fell, completing a dramatic somersault by way of celebration. The hands of fate, against all the odds, had given us just a chance.

"We should have had more faith," I murmured to Gould as we left the field for tea.

"I don't think so," he replied.

Booth-Jones' remarkable catch completely changed the tone of the match. With Zaheer back in the pavilion, the remaining Gloucestershire batsmen were solely intent on survival. As Waller and I wheeled away, fielders encircled the batsmen like birds of prey. Time was running short and only five overs remained when John Childs walked in to bat at number ten when the score was 154 for eight. It was just over a month since our encounter on the golf course near Bristol when Childs had so skilfully holed out on the eighteenth green to win the match. I was keen to take my revenge.

Childs, as you will remember, was left-handed. After he had staunchly defended a number of balls that had spun and left him,

I decided to try my arm ball, the one which goes straight on. It is often an effective way to trap a left-hander leg-before. Gould and Greig would refer to it as my 'stock' ball, whilst I regarded it as a subtle variation, indeed a surprise, which might startle the batsman.

Anyway, I bowled it at Childs from around the wicket. To my joy he was completely fooled, in fact so perplexed that instead of playing at the ball he merely shuffled across his stumps and thrust his bat above his head. The ball swung into him and struck him firmly on the shin. The whole Sussex team appealed with full voice. Surely, there could be no lucky escape for Childs this time.

Alas, it was not to be. "Not out," the umpire ruled, and that was that. My Indian taxi driver had not given me advice on how to deal with English umpires.

Shortly afterwards the match was drawn. For the second time that summer Childs had denied us victory. More to the point, we had missed the chance to extend our lead in the championship table.

*

Meanwhile, in the second Test match at Lord's, England failed to take full advantage of batting first on a dry pitch. It was Lawson this time who did the damage, by taking seven for 81. England were never able to dominate, despite a stubborn innings of 82 from Peter Willey.

Little went right for Botham, the England captain, who completed a pair of noughts in the match and, after being bowled by Ray Bright behind his legs in the second innings, was greeted by a stony cold silence from a grim-faced Lord's crowd on his return to the pavilion. At the end of a difficult year he resigned as captain.

England had yet to make an impact on a series against an Australian side that was thought to be fragile.

*

Sussex had three days free after the Gloucester game, but not Mendis, Parker and me. We had all been selected to play for the Test and County Cricket Board team against Sri Lanka at Nottingham. It was an important match for the three of us – our first glimpse of recognition from the England selectors, who were all due to be present at the match – and also for Sri Lanka, who were hoping to be granted full Test match status in the near future.

I had been asked to captain the team and was a little aprehensive at the prospect. It was one thing to captain a group of people you knew well – the Sussex team were just about getting used to me by now – but quite another to lead a bunch of relative strangers in a 'one-off' match. What on earth would they make of me? Gatting, Emburey, Downton and a young Simon Hughes from Durham University were the Middlesex contingent; Paul Allott and Paul Newman were young fast bowlers from Lancashire and Derbyshire, and Wayne Larkins and Jim Love batsmen from Northamptonshire and Yorkshire. There was lots of talent there both from within the England team and on the fringe.

I travelled up with Parker and Mendis and gave the match a lot of thought on the journey, bouncing ideas off them both as we went. It was late when we left our favourite bistro off the Old Brompton Road so unlikely that I would bump into any of my new team-mates until the next day. I still wasn't quite clear how I would handle things and went to bed unsettled and hoping for inspiration overnight.

It is a curious thing about captains that they mostly wish to make their mark and stamp their personality on proceedings at an early stage. But some try too hard, and I came into that category at Nottingham. With Sussex I always said a few words before each session we played. So I decided to give this team the same treatment.

"Let's all get together in the dressing room at 10.30 for a chat," I said to the players as we were changing for practice. I thought I detected one or two smiles. Perhaps they knew what was coming.

I was nervous before I spoke and still unsure of what I was going to say. The players sat about in various stages of undress and were probably a bit agitated themselves, as I had not yet tossed up. The chairman of the selectors, Alec Bedser, sat in a corner with fellow selector, Charlie Elliott. It was a daunting prospect.

"I know it's an unusual game and that we're all out to impress and show what we can do," I began. "But to be successful we will need to support each other, form partnerships and share the experience. That way I think we'll do even better for ourselves."

What a load of rot, I thought, as I spoke these words. We weren't really 'in it' together at all; we were in it entirely for ourselves. It was quite simply an opportunity to impress the selectors, not to show what a great team we were.

Fortunately I wasn't much put off by my undoubted gibberish. Far from it. I persevered.

"So, although we've only just assembled today, let's approach this match as a unit working together and helping each other to perform at our best. Also let's have some fun in the process and enjoy the occasion. Surely that's the way to succeed."

The longer I went on the less convincing I seemed to sound, and yet this was supposed to be my moment to make a great speech, rally the troops and impress the selectors.

That I had spoken a fair amount of drivel could not be questioned, but I knew that it was not so much the content of the talk that mattered as the manner of its delivery. I was giving it plenty of enthusiasm, energy and passion to mask and camouflage any lack of substance.

"Right then, let's go for it, and give it all we've got."

I was reaching a crescendo.

"There's heaps of talent here, let's not hold back. Nothing to fear from Sri Lanka, medium pace and spinners and a lot of shot makers."

I knew I was beginning to run out of steam starting to pace about a bit.

"Good luck everyone, all the best, have fun and we'll see where we've got to by this evening. Time to toss up, I think."

And on that dynamic note I opened the door to my left, through which I planned to make my departure, and walked straight into the airing cupboard. This broke the ice and turned a lamentable performance into a memorable one.

Bedser and Elliott remained in their corner, looking startled. Who had they selected?

Moments later, having negotiated my way out of the cupboard and onto the ground, I won the toss and chose to bat. This decision, at least, was well received, particularly by the bowlers who as always fancied a day with their feet up.

The match, which was played for the most part in muggy and overcast conditions and watched by very few locals, made well-disguised progress for the best part of two and a half days. In that time we performed well. Everyone had a chance to impress, and most had done so. But nothing of great interest really happened until the last afternoon when I took the Sri Lankans by surprise and declared setting them a target of 197 runs in three hours. In the conditions and given a short leg-side boundary, I could not have been more hospitable to our guests.

The tourists did not like the look of it. They smelt a rat, and were caught betwixt and between. On the one hand they would instinctively want to chase this absurdly easy target, but on the other they could scarcely afford to lose a prestigious match just before their application for Test match status was due to be heard. This dilemma became all the more apparent as their second innings took shape. Against some excellent pace and spin bowling Sri Lanka stumbled to 116 for five, and it actually looked as if we might bowl them out and win the match.

The rotund figure of Duleep Mendis was the last remaining recognised batsman. He was a tea taster by trade from Colombo with, as I had discovered on the Thursday night, a distinct taste for whisky, too. I also knew that he was a naturally attacking batsman and remembered how two years earlier at Horsham he had spoilt Geoff Arnold's afternoon by running down the pitch and slogging him through mid-wicket several times. Arnold's language which could be strong at the best of times included the expletive "you curry muncher," which was not uttered as a term of endearment.

And yet here was Mendis in Nottingham, uncharacteristically blocking every ball and not making a very good job of it. He probably felt it was his duty to save the game with national honour depending on it. But such ungainly defensive play certainly made for dire cricket.

I was fielding at slip and also keen to make my mark.

"Why don't you play your natural game and attack the bowling?" I suggested to him.

Mendis thought for a second.

"Your fielders are set too deep for me to do that."

"Why don't you put the fielders where you want?" I replied, aware that these were unorthodox tactics.

"Are you sure?" he said with an air of distrust.

"Quite sure."

So Mendis set the field. Mid-wicket came in, mid-on moved round a bit and he adjusted extra cover.

Emburey, the bowler, was dumbfounded by these goings-on.

"Are we still taking this match seriously?" he asked.

I explained to Emburey that I wanted to invite Mendis to play his shots, which he was prepared to do if the field came in a bit.

"If you could just toss it up a little," I suggested, "that might encourage him."

Emburey muttered something under his breath – I think it was about captains – and went back to his mark.

The tactics worked. Mendis began to play with much more confidence, dancing down the pitch to Emburey and striking the bowling into the vacant mid-wicket area. Emburey looked astonished. He was not used to such rough and disrespectful treatment. Mendis was warming to the task, and the turning point came when he clouted Emburey for three fours and a six in one over.

Not for the first time I had got carried away by my own enthusiasm and, by the time I tried to regain control and set the fields myself, it was too late. The match was beyond repair.

But what I think really miffed Emburey was that I brought myself on to bowl at the other end from him and immediately posted fielders around the boundary, particularly protecting the deep mid-wicket area. I proceeded to bowl rather fast and unambitiously, not joining in the fun at all.

"Typical," jested Emburey. "So much for the team talk. 'We're all in it together' and all that sharing stuff."

Although we've laughed about it many times since, I've never quite been allowed to forget those two hours. Mendis, our tea-tasting, whisky-drinking friend from Colombo, was unstoppable. Despite losing seven wickets, Sri Lanka won the game with three overs to spare and, I have to admit, I felt a strange satisfaction in the result. It didn't matter to me as much as perhaps it should have done.

There was a minor pitch invasion at the end. A solitary Sri Lankan, waving his country's flag, raced onto the field, all smiles and joy, and embraced Mendis by trying to wrap his arms around him. Not an easy task.

"What a hero," I said to Mendis as we left the field in dingy light. "Colombo will be buzzing tonight."

As I passed the Sri Lankan dressing room, their manager rushed out and flung his arms around me, taking me by surprise and knocking me off balance.

"Oh thank you, thank you," he gasped, quite overcome with emotion. "You have done a great thing for our cricket and should be granted the freedom of Colombo, I tell you. We are so grateful."

Never had I been so popular after losing a game. Even my own team – except Emburey, possibly – thought it was rather fun. A few days later the Sri Lankans, while they were still in England, were granted the official Test status they so much desired and indeed deserved.

CHAMPIONSHIP TABLE – 7 JULY

		Played	Points
1.	Hampshire	10	113
2.	Somerset	10	102
3.	Surrey	10	100
4.	Sussex	10	95

Paul Parker

Chapter Nine

See You in the Bar, Garth

v Somerset: at Taunton, July 11,13,14
v Surrey: at Hove, July 15,16,17
v Warwickshire: at Hove, July 18,20,21

From Nottingham it was back to the next county championship match against Somerset at Taunton. Somerset were, at that time, one of the strongest sides in the country and included the combined talents of Viv Richards, Joel Garner and, of course, Ian Botham. We were still without Imran, but le Roux was fit again and we now badly needed a win to keep us up with the leaders.

Botham gave us his usual great welcome. Irrepressible as ever and showing no signs of his recent upset at Lord's, he had particularly taken le Roux to heart, another big man who bowled fast and batted with gusto. "I'll show you around Taunton," Botham said to him. "A good evening out, that's what we'll have." Le Roux concurred, little knowing what this might mean.

The pitch was green and bouncy. It wasn't long before Somerset were in real trouble against the seam-bowling skills of Arnold and Greig. Botham came in, hit a six and then had a huge heave at a ball from Greig which he missed and was conclusively bowled. With a shrug of his shoulders and a dismissive swing of his bat he trudged back to the pavilion. There was a good Saturday crowd and, as he was approaching the boundary fence, a frustrated spectator broke the silence by shouting at him, "You're rubbish, Botham."

This was too much for the great man. He reacted instantly, by smashing open the pavilion gate. Bat, pads and gloves were flung to the ground and, with the words "I'm going to get that bastard," he made off towards where he thought the spectator was sitting. There then followed a chase in which the frightened viewer was pursued by Botham all around the ground and eventually right out of it.

*

I had my own physical encounter with Botham the following year when, playing at Taunton in the first match of the season in April, I was opening the batting and facing the bowling of Hallam

Moseley, all arms and legs and national health spectacles which from time to time would fly off his nose and land disconcertingly on the pitch in front of him. Our innings had only just got under way when he bowled me a wide ball outside the off-stump which, in the freezing weather, I swished at full of hope. I did make contact but only with the bottom of the bat from where the ball looped up gently in the direction of Botham at second slip, offering him a simple catch.

Botham stood there stock still in three jumpers, as if frozen to the spot, with hands characteristically clenched on his knees. He seemed to be looking my way and yet never moved. The ball continued its journey uninterrupted, until it was brought to an abrupt halt when it collided with Botham's delicate lower frame and abruptly awoke him from his dream.

"Aaaagh." He hit the ground with a massive groan and a thump. Clearly he was in agony and quite inconsolable to boot. Removing him from the field was not easy and required the might of several Somerset players as well as le Roux, Phillipson and Arnold who emerged from the pavilion to help carry him off.

*

Back to 1981 and Somerset never quite recovered from Botham's dismissal. Le Roux, Arnold and Greig took just 25 overs to skittle them for 104. Even Richards failed.

Initially, we didn't find it easy going either. Booth-Jones was welcomed by two very fast bouncers from Botham, followed by an inviting swinging half-volley which he steered straight to Richards in the gully. Tim sat for a good half an hour in his corner of the dressing room murmuring, "What an honour – caught Richards, bowled Botham, 0. What an honour." It was good to see someone so easily pleased.

Not for the first time it was the bowlers who got us out of trouble when we batted. Phillipson, Arnold, le Roux and Waller all chipped in. "Always getting you batters out of trouble," Arnold would remind us. Le Roux had had a particularly good day, wickets in the morning followed by a half century in the evening.

Botham put his head round our dressing-room door and reminded our big fast bowler of their evening plans.

"See you in the bar, Garth."

"Look forward to it," Garth shouted back.

*

The next day was Sunday so we switched our attention to defending our position at the top of the table. To relax the nerves and soothe the mind, I went to church in the morning with Parker and Phillipson.

St Mary Magdalene is the larger of the two churches in Taunton that are visible from the ground; the other is St James into whose churchyard balls are frequently peppered. It's not a big hit for the strong men of Somerset but we chose St Mary's, which is more like a drive and a pitch shot from the ground, and joined a lively congregation for the morning service. Afterwards, we strolled contentedly to the ground spiritually uplifted and ready for the day ahead.

The first person we saw there was Botham. "Fancy a throwing competition?" he shouted at Parker. "You, me, Garth and anyone else mad enough to have a go."

Parker couldn't resist the challenge and, given that he had a magnificent throwing arm, he rather fancied his chances and it seemed as good a way of warming up for the match as any. So for the next half hour Somerset took on Sussex at throwing the cricket ball, a sport more familiar to an old-fashioned school sports day than a Sunday morning at Taunton prior to a cricket match.

Members of the crowd bravely judged the distances as balls flew this way and that and on balance, Sussex just about came out on top, which was surprising considering the instinctive nature of the Somerset supporters. Parker out-threw everyone by a distance. Botham was in fine form too but even he was not in the same league. He did, however, seem remarkably chirpy despite his late night out with le Roux, whom we found later in the dressing room looking pale and with a strong cup of coffee at his side. He had clearly caught the full force of an evening out with Botham and was now suffering from its considerable aftershock.

On the field it was not our day. From the outset we were in trouble and never really recovered. Le Roux did manage to score 18 brave runs, his head booming with protest after every shot, and we finished with a meagre score of just 154 to defend.

We did at least make a gesture of defiance. Le Roux trapped Richards lbw for 46, which was a mighty achievement in the circumstances. With Richards out of the way, there was always hope. I do remember one year when I managed to deceive him with a flighty ball which he tried to hit out of the ground, missed and was bowled. Le Roux ran at top speed all the way from the deep square leg boundary to congratulate me. "Captain," he said, "that's like catching a twenty pound salmon first cast." I glowed with pride. It never happened again.

Our only minor triumph before the end was to run out Botham without his facing a ball. 'He stalked from the field doom-laden, like the Mayor of Casterbridge on a bad day,' wrote David Green in *The Times*. This was but small consolation. We lost and were dislodged from the top of the table.

*

On the Monday it was the turn of Botham to get his own back with a whirlwind innings of 72 in just 17 overs. 'Unhelmeted and uninhibited,' John Woodcock wrote, 'he waded into the Sussex attack, hitting twelve fours and a towering six.'

We could see the change in him already, now he had been relieved of the England captaincy, but would it make a difference in the third Test match at Headingley coming up on Thursday?

Somerset were finally dismissed for 367, with le Roux taking eight for 107. We were left with the teasing task of scoring 239 to win. A brilliant partnership of 131 between Booth-Jones and Parker, who scored his fourth hundred of the season, paved the way to a victory by six wickets This took Sussex into joint first place in the county championship with Nottinghamshire.

*

Relentlessly, day after day, the matches rolled on, one game absorbed into another, and with no time to think or reflect between them. Cricket cases had to be packed up and lugged from pavilion to car and back into another pavilion. County cricket was a giddy whirl of activity, which left normal life behind and where relaxation became the car radio on the way from one destination to another.

My travelling companions on Tuesday and Friday nights, the days on which games ended, were introduced to my favourite programmes. *'Brain of Britain 1981'*, with Robert Robinson in the chair, was one of them. We considered it a major triumph to get a question right before the contestant and on real red-letter days we got three in a row and 'a round of applause', but that was very rare. Colin Wells was our star performer. He seemed to know things which others didn't.

Then there was *'Just a Minute'* with Nicholas Parsons in the chair. Many a mile was covered while Kenneth Williams, Clement Freud, Derek Nimmo and Peter Jones, entertained us as they tried to speak on a subject – "gobstoppers" perhaps, or "how I choose my friends" or "spiders" – for just a minute. We loved it.

'Pick of the Week' with Margaret Howard was another favourite, closely followed by *'Any Questions'*, chaired by David Jacobs. These programmes provided the county cricketer with the chance to catch up with what was going on in the outside world and far away from cricket grounds. "Should garages start selling petrol by the litre rather than the gallon?" Weighty matters such as this were debated and helped us on our way up and down the motorways.

We travelled back from our successful encounter at Taunton to Hove for a rain-ruined match against Surrey in which the only notable feature was the return of Imran Khan with his ankle repaired. It was very good to have him back despite his being at times a man with unexpected anxieties.

"Oh, no!" he confessed. "Oh, no! I cannot play that Pat Pocock. He is such a good bowler." He would look over towards le Roux. "What should I do, Garth, where should I hit him?"

"Just smash him over the top, man, like you do the others," le Roux replied impatiently, while the rest of us looked on astonished. We all had great respect for Pocock but, as a slow bowler and so not likely to hurt us, he scarcely gave us sleepless nights.

Khan, caught Lynch, bowled Pocock 19, the scorebook read. Mid-off took the catch.

"I should have followed through," was all Imran said as he took off his pads. "That Pocock is such a good bowler."

It made no difference. We had played ourselves into a promising position with a large first innings lead when the rain came and washed out the final afternoon's cricket.

Meanwhile at Headingley, thanks to Dyson, Hughes and Yallop, Australia were amassing a sizeable score, 401 for 9 declared, and dominating the first two days of the Test match. Gooch and Boycott survived on the Friday night to fight another day.

*

Warwickshire followed Surrey to Hove. Only a small crowd turned up on the Saturday to watch, presumably because most were torturing themselves in front of the television where England, who collapsed in their first innings for 174, followed on and then lost Gooch again in the evening.

Warwickshire made 249, and Sussex's reply featured another unusual incident involving Booth-Jones.

Mendis had cracked three majestic fours before falling to the bowling of Gladstone Small. Soon afterwards Small, with his tail up, bowled Tim a sharp bouncer. Taken completely by surprise, only at the very last moment did he throw back his head to evade the lethal missile. The ball missed him by a whisker but just flicked his spectacles, balanced precariously on his nose, and it was they, rather than the ball, that flew through to Geoff Humpage, the wicket-keeper. He caught them gleefully, and there followed a tremendous appeal with the spectacles thrown triumphantly into the air in celebration. For a while the fielders wouldn't return the spectacles to Booth-Jones, who could only stand there blinking helplessly.

I watched this episode as non-striker, next to the umpire, Arthur Jepson. "What's going on? Stop mucking about," he said, as the spectacles were passed around the slips.

Tim's glasses seemed to have a mind of their own. Perched on the end of his nose, he peered over the top of them somewhat disconcertingly to such an extent that the players' wives and girlfriends were never quite sure whether he was peering down their cleavage or looking them in the face. Quite vexing.

By the Monday afternoon things had gone from bad to worse at Headingley, and England were staring an innings defeat in the face. Brearley, Gower and Gatting had all gone cheaply, and only Boycott and Willey pulled things together for any time at all. But when Boycott departed, after a three and a half hour vigil, lbw to

Alderman, the game was up. Not long afterwards England were teetering on the brink of defeat at 135 for seven, with humiliation and embarrassment coming into view.

Back at Hove our own performance seemed to mirror that of England. Whenever an England wicket fell, a gloomy announcement would be made over the ground's loudspeakers, and we invariably lost a wicket too, as if in sympathy. The damage was done by Warwickshire's bespectacled left-arm spinner Dilip Doshi. A naturally unathletic cricketer, he had been limping about all day suffering from a strained calf muscle and so was not called upon to bowl by Amiss, the Warwickshire captain, until mid-afternoon when, fastidious as ever over his field placing, Doshi took three wickets for seven runs in a menacing spell that bamboozled the Sussex lower order. We were bowled out for 208, conceding a first innings lead of 41.

As we left the pavilion for Warwickshire's second innings, it was clear that Botham, now accompanied by Graham Dilley, was intent upon having one last heroic blast at Alderman and Lillee. Hughes set attacking fields, and Botham lashed out at anything within reach. This was Botham the dare-devil, the outrageous; no wonder that unfortunate man at Taunton had hurried out of the ground so quickly when pursued by him. He was now on the rampage and seemingly unstoppable. Botham and Dilley both flayed the bowling and scattered the field in as thrilling a display as imaginable.

It was not easy for anyone to concentrate on our match. A ripple of applause rang round Hove when England's 200 came up. It wouldn't last long, we all thought. Then there was further applause for Botham's fifty. The crowd scarcely noticed that Imran and le Roux were celebrating England's revival by reducing Warwickshire to 77 for five.

"England have taken the lead," shouted a triumphant voice from the deckchairs. Botham's hundred, Dilley's fifty, the hundred partnership, they were all celebrated enthusiastically in the evening sunshine at Hove. When Dilley finally departed, bowled by Alderman for 56, the two had added 117 runs in 80 minutes. To look after Botham, as Dilley had done for all that time, was some achievement – every bit as demanding as a night out with him in Taunton.

His replacement, Chris Old, another left-hander, kept up the good work by adding 67 more priceless runs with Botham. But England were still only 124 runs ahead at close of play, with nine wickets down and only Willis to keep Botham company. Surely it was nothing like enough, just a gesture of defiance, but at least England might now go down fighting.

In the morning Botham and Willis increased England's lead to 130 while at Hove Sussex were frustrated by drizzle sweeping in off the sea and so we all watched the cricket from Leeds on the television instead. Botham, following up his remarkable innings of 149 not out, picked up the first wicket to fall, Wood caught by Taylor for 10. There then followed a lull when Australia began to take the initiative. The turning point for England came when Brearley switched Willis and bowled him from the Kirkstall Lane end from where he was able to come in down the hill and with the wind behind him.

It was a brave decision. Many fast bowlers, including Willis I suspect, felt uncomfortable running down that hill. Frequently they lost rhythm and no-balls were often the result. Brearley had to take that chance. But he was immediately rewarded when Willis got a ball to spit and rear off a length at Trevor Chappell and Taylor took the catch. Kim Hughes, the Australian captain, followed almost immediately and then Yallop. Four wickets down at lunch, and it seemed to us at Hove that Allan Border's was now the crucial wicket needed, even though Dyson had been batting defiantly from the outset.

But we could watch no more. The rain had relented, and we had our own match to play.

We had just got out onto the field with the players ready to do battle, when a cheer went up round the ground.

"Border's out," somebody shouted.

"How?" we shouted back.

"Bowled by Old, chopped it on."

I felt I was playing in two matches at the same time, one physically and the other in spirit. While we were trying to beat Warwickshire at Hove, my mind kept drifting up to Headingley to confuse the issue.

"Play," boomed Jepson, and we were on our way.

As if inspired by England's heroic and unexpected fight back we produced a small sensation of our own at Hove. Le Roux fairly stormed in to bowl that afternoon and proceeded to take a hat-trick, dismissing Ferreira and Small off the last two balls of one over and Amiss off the first ball of the next.

The spectators hardly knew which match to concentrate on with wickets falling so frequently in both. At Hove, Warwickshire contrived to lose their last five wickets for just 10 runs in 25 minutes, which left us a target of 168 to win.

We came off the field just in time to see Rod Marsh and Geoff Lawson getting out. The rest is now glorious history. Willis roared in down that hill, arms pumping, jaw jutting out, staring in front of him as if in a trance. His final, and eighth wicket, was as comprehensive as it could be, shattering Bright's stumps and conluded what was, without question, Willis's finest hour.

Botham's innings for me summed up his life and how he chose to live it. Brave, almost crazy, on the edge – but what fun. Everyone had of course played their part. Chris Old, who took over at the Football Stand end from Willey, bowled a steady and calming spell at a crucial time in support of the main heroes. And Willey bowled three overs of sensible off-spin to keep the ship on course. It all helped.

But the most extraordinary feature was the performance of Mike Brearley. It was scarcely two months since we had been plodding about together in the mud at Lord's while he tried to persuade me that conditions were fit enough for a ten-over match. He could surely never then have anticipated such a remarkable turn of events – nor could anyone else. For three and a half days things could not have gone much worse for Brearley and his team before, for no apparent reason, the tide of events began to turn. With cricket, the unexpected can lurk behind any corner.

Where did the balance between luck and skill lie? Was there something in Brearley's manner that gave Botham and Willis the freedom to play as they did? I wonder. And how did Brearley retain his control and composure on that final day? He must have known he had wounded the Australians, but how hard it must have been to time his offensive and go in for the kill.

I believe that a jockey, when driving his mount to the finishing post, has to achieve a perfect balance to ensure that his horse runs rhythmically and with momentum. Brearley achieved this in the field at Headingley. The Australians froze amidst the pressure, and all of a sudden the course of the summer was dramatically changed.

As we settled down to chase the runs at Hove, we watched the television scenes of the crowd at Headingley waving Union Jacks and chanting patriotically, and all this just a few days before the Royal Wedding.

With the excitement over in the Test match, Parker steered us successfully to the required target and a triumph which took us into a clear lead at the top of the championship table.

CHAMPIONSHIP TABLE – 21 JULY

		Played	Points
1.	Sussex	13	145
2.	Hampshire	12	142
3.	Nottinghamshire	13	141
4.	Surrey	13	132

Gehan Mendis

Chapter Ten

I Promise

v Surrey: at Guildford, July 29,30,31

"Make sure you're not late this evening," Mary-Lou said to me as I stood at the front door of our cottage in Henfield. "The party starts at 6.30 so see if you can get back as soon as possible."

Georgina, now six months old, was perched on her hip. Even she seemed to sense that July 29th was an exciting day, and indeed it was. At last, after the seemingly eternal build-up, the Royal Wedding day had arrived.

"Have a lovely day," I said, kissing them goodbye. "I promise I'll leave as soon as the cricket is over."

"You'd better," Mary-Lou added.

The reason for the hint of authority that I detected in her voice was the street party which she was helping to organise in the lane just outside our cottage. Elaborate plans, about which I knew nothing, had been made. All the locals were expecting to be there, and it had been made quite clear to me that cricket was no excuse for absence.

The sun was shining. It was high summer, and I was in good spirits as I drove to Guildford. In the week since the Warwickshire match at Hove, we had beaten them again – comfortably – at Edgbaston in the NatWest Trophy. We were now second in the championship table behind Nottinghamshire, with Surrey, our opponents, in fourth place.

As a child, I had always thought of Guildford as a Christmas shopping town rather than a cricketing venue. I connected it with cold, dark evenings, roasted chestnuts, mince pies and carol singers while we stumped up and down the steep hills buying presents. Nostalgic though that was, cricket was infinitely preferable.

I won the toss and batted. The good news for Sussex was that Sylvester Clarke had an infected shinbone and so was unable to play. Clarke was a particularly mean and hostile West Indian fast bowler, and his absence was the source of quiet rejoicing amongst the Sussex players.

But we still had to contend with Robin Jackman. He was never injured, ever present in every Surrey side I played against. I had great admiration for his tenacity and skill, whilst he had the highest regard for my forward defensive shot. He never expected me to play an attacking stroke of any sort and would inquire tenderly after my health if such an attempt was ever made. I frequently blocked half-volleys, if nothing else to reassure him that I had not lost my sense of perspective. The banter was constant. He never stopped talking and nor did I.

The morning session took on a familiar pattern. Mendis was dominant and forceful as usual, while I nicked and nudged at the other end and chatted with Jackman. Despite the Royal Wedding there was still a good holiday crowd and for an hour and ten minutes I kept them on the edge of their seats by scoring 14 runs, all in singles.

For the players, Guildford is the perfect place for watching cricket. Its pavilion is right behind the bowler's arm and, upstairs, the balcony offers a fine view of the ground. It was from here beside one of the large windows that I settled down later, with a television at my side, to watch the cricket and wedding ceremony simultaneously. By chance, I had timed my dismissal rather well and not missed much of the service. I confess I do have a weakness for pageantry: royal occasions, trooping the colour and the like. We're so very good at it in this country. If playing soldiers were an Olympic sport we'd surely win a gold medal. The commentary was entertaining too so I spent a happy morning watching the wedding to my left on the television set and Booth-Jones and Parker batting to my right.

The players, whilst waiting to go into bat, were half-watching too. Ian Gould brushed past me.

"Gorgeous," he said, "a little darling."

Imran was next man in, nervously pacing up and down in his pads like a panther waiting to be fed.

"She is beautiful," he conceded, "but not my type." He added, by way of explanation, "Too young."

We weren't convinced. He would have snapped her up any day, given half a chance. The dreaming ended when Parker ran down the wicket to Pocock, missed the ball and was stumped by a yard.

"Oh no, not Pocock again," Imran said, as he placed his floppy hat onto his head before making his way out in to bat. I don't know why he went on so much about Pocock because he played him perfectly well and, less than two hours later, was back in the pavilion having made 92 exciting runs.

Weddings always leave me a little tearful and this one was no exception. Rather charmingly, the bride and groom got their vows slightly muddled, and later Kiri Te Kanawa sang so beautifully that a lump stayed in my throat for a good two overs.

It was a glorious ceremony and when the Prince and Princess of Wales stood together afterwards smiling happily on the steps of St Paul's Cathedral, it seemed the whole nation was on their side.

*

In the meantime we made a very acceptable 302 all out and, after we had bowled a few overs at Surrey that evening, I left the field hurriedly at close of play, keen to return quickly to the Henfield street party.

There I found things were in full swing. Flags and bunting waving, tables and chairs set up, people everywhere. I never knew we had so many neighbours; heaps of food and drink, music playing. A worthy celebration.

"You're late," Mary-Lou said.

"I came as quickly as I could," I replied apologetically, "but you know what it's like."

"Well now you're here, take Georgie for a while, that would be a help."

Georgina was thrust into my arms, and Mary-Lou bustled off to organise something else. The village was having fun. A hundred and fifty, maybe two hundred people had come along to celebrate. It seemed like most of Henfield.

The light of the summer evening gradually faded and, with the South Downs silhouetted against the sky, the corn gently rustling in the breeze, the candles flickering to and fro and the River Adur meandering its way through the valley, one could not help but feel that Sussex was a very good place to be.

*

Surrey batted for much of the second day and reached 311. But the match changed dramatically on the third morning, when we found ourselves reeling hopelessly at 46 for seven and our championship ambitions seemingly going up in smoke. David Thomas and Jackman did the damage. Our tail-enders, led by Paul Phillipson, managed to make a partial recovery and take our score past 100, but it was still nowhere near enough.

In the gathering gloom of the evening, Pakistani all-rounder Intikhab Alam, 'sane and saintly as a Buddha', steered Surrey safely home with the minimum of fuss

Our second championship defeat saw us drop to third in the table.

In that mad run chase at Tunbridge Wells, we had been the moral victors, but here at Guildford we were comprehensively outplayed.

CHAMPIONSHIP TABLE – 31 JULY

		Played	Points
1.	Nottinghamshire	15	164
2.	Surrey	14	155
3.	Sussex	14	153
4.	Hampshire	12	142

Ian Gould

Chapter Eleven
The Chapel of Rest

v Leicestershire: at Leicester, August 1,3,4

When you fall off a horse, the best thing, I am told, is to get straight back on again; if you don't, you might lose confidence in riding altogether. For Sussex, happily, we had little chance to let the Surrey defeat sap our confidence. We were back in the saddle at Leicester the very next day, and I was shaking hands with another captain, Roger Tolchard, with whom I tossed up for the start of a new match. We would now have to dig deeply into our reserves of energy and enthusiasm if we were to maintain momentum.

But the country's interest was firmly focused on Birmingham, not Leicester. England had once again been thrown onto the back foot by Australia who were as resilient as ever after their shock at Leeds. On an unreliable pitch England had conceded a first innings lead of 69 and then, in their second innings on the Saturday, were brushed aside by the left-arm spin of Bright, who took five wickets.

In the meantime we spent a long day in the field, our limbs increasingly achey and minds dulled by the batting of John Steele. He laboured his way to three runs short of a century, and there seemed no way of breaking through his resolute and impeccable defence. Oddly, I was full of admiration for Steele; here was a batsman after my own heart and of similar technique.

The crowd, as was the case not long ago at Hove, was far more interested in the Test match. Australia needed only 151 runs to win with a full two days remaining. Surely lightning could not possibly strike twice in a fortnight? When, by Sunday afternoon, Australia had reached 105 for four Brearley must have been at the end of his tether and desperately trying to recapture the magic of Headingley. Then, out of the blue, Emburey bowled a brute of a ball to Border which turned and lifted sharply from a length and Gatting took the catch. The breakthrough had been made, but was it too late?

With the pitch untrustworthy and taking spin, Brearley might easily have turned to his other slow bowler, Willey, to complement the accuracy and cunning of Emburey. But no, with just a handful of runs to play with, he threw the ball to Botham, who eagerly paced out his run-up at the city end of the ground in preparation to bowl.

This was a last throw of the dice. By his standards Botham had contributed little in the match so far. But now he roared in and bowled faster than ever, pitching the ball up and swinging it sinuously. Australia had no answer to this onslaught and lost their last five wickets for just seven runs. Botham himself took all five for one run in 28 balls and so destroyed Australia for the second time in two weeks.

It appeared he had never looked back since that night out with le Roux in Taunton.

Amidst all the hullabaloo at Birmingham it was as much as we could do to keep our minds on the job at Leicester. Great cheers went up from the crowd every time another wicket fell. Kent, Marsh, Bright, Lillee, Alderman, they were all out in quick succession.

*

In the Sunday League match, we had problems of our own against the West Indian fast bowler, Andy Roberts, who for the last seven years had been the scourge of many a terrified English batsman. He bowled with a fearsome look on his face and a cold stare in his eye. Fortunately, by 1981, helmets had become fashionable. The intimidating nature of Kerry Packer's World Series Cricket in 1977 had been the catalyst for this and, since then, helmets had crept as insidiously into the game as sponsored cars. Now, both are an essential part of the professional cricketer's life.

In the early days helmets were worn somewhat apologetically and self-consciously. Brearley, for example, used his normal cricket cap with protection cleverly sewn in. Amiss went the whole hog and wore a white crash helmet like a motor cyclist. Some players wore a visor in front of their faces. For all that I was a reluctant helmet user at first despite being hit on the head fairly regularly.

It took a fierce ball from Jeff Thomson in 1985 to convince me fully of their need. Sussex were playing the Australians at Hove. We had batted well and lasted long enough for them to take the second new ball. First Thomson bowled me a loosener, a wide swinging half-volley to which I played an ugly shot for four runs over gully.

He looked at me in disgust and muttered a few choice Australian words, which I didn't fully pick up but I could tell he wasn't happy.

He tore in menacingly for his next ball with a look of thunder in his face and, with his disconcertingly slingy action, unleashed a short and venomous delivery, which I thought I had covered. Unfortunately the ball collided painfully with my face, disturbing one or two teeth in the process. Brave to the last, I collapsed to the ground in a heap and, encouraged by Keppler Wessels who was rather surprisingly playing for Australia, decided to declare the Sussex innings closed.

When I reached the pavilion, I noticed our newly appointed chaplain standing on the top of the steps leading to the dressing room. Just the man, I thought, to minister to my suffering. He greeted me with a warm smile, which I tried unsuccessfully to reciprocate.

"Bad luck, old man," he said.

"Well, what do you think?" I mumbled through my swollen gums, hoping to attract some words of comfort.

He looked at my wounded face sympathetically before giving me some profound advice.

"If you'd gone back a bit further, got your hands up higher and kept your head still, I think you'd have played the ball a lot better."

When I returned from Casualty in Brighton, I asked Thomson to autograph my blood-stained batting gloves as a souvenir and somewhat unwillingly concluded that helmets had become a necessity.

Back at Leicester we were still in with a good chance to win the Sunday League, so a strong performance was really important. Roberts fairly raced in off his shortened run-up but, despite removing Gould, Khan, Greig and Wells in quick succession, could not prevent our winning by three wickets off the last ball but one. Combined with a win the previous weekend at Ebbw Vale against Glamorgan, we now remained hard on the heels of Essex at the top of the table.

*

As our game with Leicestershire in the championship progressed on the Monday, Tolchard and I indulged in the already common practice of match-fixing. The weather was hot, the pitch was good and the outfield fast; this was all about the art of negotiation.

As it turned out on the Tuesday afternoon, we stuck pretty well to our deal. Tolchard set us 264 runs to win in around 55 overs, with just a hint of spin now to be abstracted from the wearing pitch. The match was set up for the run chase. The target was not many more than the one we had to pursue at Tunbridge Wells but with twice the number of overs to play with. This was a serious proposition and required some tactical thought.

Gould and Mendis should open, I reasoned. I had scored a hundred in the first innings which, on the law of averages, was unlikely to be repeated. "Then let's have our normal order with le Roux and Phillipson at the ready in case of emergency," I said. I went on to stress all the usual things. "Good start, look for singles, run hard, talk to each other, play your shots, don't get out." We all watched from the balcony.

Mendis and Gould did indeed give us a magnificent start, both being particularly severe on the two young fast bowlers, Agnew and Parsons. They rattled up 59 runs in just nine overs before Gould's dazzling display came to an end. While the batting faltered around him, Mendis played another innings of rare quality, entertaining and aggressive, against both pace and spin. He dominated proceedings while batsmen came and went at the other end. When the score was 140 for three, Greig was bowled by Nick Cook, the left-arm spinner, and Imran went in to replace him.

Greig returned to the pavilion as dejected as any batsman who has just got out. This was understandable for dismissal is so very final, and accordingly the atmosphere back in the dressing room needs to be both respectful and quiet. It is as if, for a moment, there has been a death in the family. Silence reigns while the stricken batsman removes gloves and pads and recovers during an important and necessary period of mourning. One moment you're batting, the next you're out – dead, banished to the pavilion and often humiliated. It's a horrid shock, and a bereavement which only time can heal.

We spoke in hushed tones while Greig gradually came back to life. He was offered a drink by the wretched twelfth man whose role in such circumstances is not dissimilar to that of an undertaker –

sombre, caring and considerate – not an easy job for a professional cricketer.

The match proceeded peacefully until Imran was drawn into a drive by Cook and caught at slip. 164 for five and more respectful silence in the dressing room.

*

There was often drama attached to Imran's batting. A year later at Lord's, I remember, he was particularly agitated while awaiting his turn to bat against Middlesex.

"Shall I hook Daniel or shall I duck?" he kept asking himself. He turned to le Roux for advice. "Garth, what shall I do?"

Le Roux and Imran had been inseparable since coming together at Sussex. Although quite different temperamentally, they were well suited in many ways. They shared rooms, travelled in the same car and often went out on the town together. Le Roux was lying on his back in the huge Lord's changing room, reading a Wilbur Smith novel while Imran tried again.

"What do you think, Garth, shall I hook or shall I duck?"

"Don't be silly, man. Duck, of course."

"Why?" asked Imran.

"Because whenever you hook you always get out, stupid."

It was a tetchy exchange and Imran had no real answer to this. Then another Sussex wicket fell and he was in. Down the stairs he went, through the Long Room and out onto the field. Lord's, Imran's favourite ground in the world. The score was an unpromising 49 for 3, chasing 262 to win. Imran joined Parker at the crease and, for a while, all went well against Emburey and Edmonds, the best pair of spinners in the country at the time. Imran played himself in sensibly, and it was not long before he was into his stride and beginning to bat fluently and with a degree of comfort.

As it happened the tea interval was fast approaching, and the score had reached 100 when Brearley, directing things quietly from slip, suddenly clapped his hands and signalled to Wayne Daniel that he wanted him to loosen up for a bowl. It was a strange decision because there appeared to be only time for one more over before tea. Daniel would need to get ready quickly, and so began to put himself through a series of contorted warm-up exercises.

We had learnt, however, never to underestimate Brearley. Before Daniel bowled, the England captain took a lot of trouble over setting the field and carefully placed two men – his best fielders, Slack and Barlow – in the deep on the leg-side boundary. Imran eyed them suspiciously.

"Shall I hook or shall I duck?" He was clearly still concerned by this vexing problem.

Daniel pitched up the first three balls of the over and Imran played serenely forward, looking perfectly at ease. It was about then that our twelfth man, Alan Willows, wheeled a large trolley into the dressing room laden with sandwiches, cakes and a huge pot of tea. The players, diverted by the prospect of food, took their minds off the cricket for a moment and made a bee-line for the best sandwiches. Cricketers are scavengers at heart.

There were just three balls left before tea. Daniel thumped the first of them in short and Imran, despite his best intentions, could not resist the temptation. The ball was on to him a shade quicker than he thought; his head rocked back as he made contact, and the ball spiralled high into the air towards those fielders on the leg-side boundary.

"Oh no," Imran groaned as he set off for an optimistic single while Barlow placed himself carefully beneath the ball and took the catch. Imran was out for 40.

Suddenly there was a hush in the dressing room as the team prepared itself for an uncomfortable period of gloom and despondency. Players grabbed their sandwiches and slunk off quietly into the background, not wishing to draw attention to themselves. I, by now a captain of some experience, kept a low profile. It was left to our gallant twelfth man to handle the crisis. With heavy hearts, we awaited Imran's return.

After what seemed like an age, the door was pushed open and in came the two batsmen. They were greeted by respectful silence, only broken by the sound of the poor twelfth man, clumsily trying to pour tea into the cups without making a noise. Imran sat with his head in gloved hands whispering, "no, no" over and over again.

He was inconsolable, and I was wondering from my corner how to break this spell of cheerlessness before the after-tea session of batting began.

Then le Roux, who had not yet looked up from his Wilbur Smith, raised his head and fixing his eyes upon his friend, Imran, shook his head in sympathy and said in his gentle South African voice, "You know, I think our government may be right at times, you blacks will never learn." And he returned to his book.

There was complete silence and nobody spoke.

Quelled as we were by the presence of death and numbed by le Roux's shocking remark, we watched Imran whose face gradually but visibly began to break into an oafish grin, followed by much laughter.

The ice had been broken and the funeral was over.

"But I thought it was just right for hooking," Imran said.

Nobody was listening.

*

At Leicester, the chapel of rest had been busy since Imran's dismissal and wickets continued to fall. Barclay, le Roux and Phillipson, had all been in and out. Only Mendis, seemingly unstoppable, had been able to cope with the bowling of Cook.

We crept nearer and nearer to the target. With just two wickets left, six runs were needed from the final over. Arnold managed a single. Then from the third ball Mendis went for a big hit and was stumped, out for a magnificent 137. Off the fourth ball Waller scrambled another single.

That left the ball firmly in Arnold's court. My dependable right-hand man, the leader of our training sessions, the dispenser of sage advice and no slouch with the bat, either.

Four runs to win. Cook bowled the fifth ball of the final over to Arnold who had a mighty swipe and missed. One ball to go. The odds were definitely against us now. Another huge swish. Again he missed but this time there was the unwelcome sound of broken stumps which, as it had done at Tunbridge Wells, brought the match to its conclusion with the last ball.

A second defeat in a row. We were now fourth in the table.

CHAMPIONSHIP TABLE – 4 AUGUST

		Played	*Points*
1.	Nottinghamshire	16	187
2.	Essex	15	163
3.	Surrey	15	160
4.	Sussex	15	157

Imran Khan

Chapter Twelve
Johnny, I Want to Bowl

v Kent: at Eastbourne, August 8,10,11
v Derbyshire: at Eastbourne, August 12,13,14

Our losing streak continued. We were bundled out of the quarter finals of the NatWest Trophy by Essex, captained once again by Fletcher, who, in my view, came a close second to Brearley for cunning and resourcefulness.

Next it was down to Eastbourne and its traditional cricket week at the Saffrons – ice creams, croquet, fluffy old ladies and seagulls – it provided a most welcome interlude and, with a circus pitched in the adjacent field, was a haven of tranquillity and just the right place in which to recharge our batteries. They had gone rather flat since playing Surrey at Guildford.

The pitch for our return match against Kent was bright green and covered with a generous layer of unmown grass. Influenced by the rumours that the Trent Bridge lawn-mower had scarcely seen the light of day all summer, I had paid a visit to the Saffrons two days earlier and introduced myself to its new groundsman, Ken McLaren.

As luck would have it, he had been in his day a formidable fast bowler and so, when I suggested that he too might use the mower sparingly, he concurred quite jauntily. He was one of those who held the view that bowlers should not be treated as second-class citizens.

Nowadays such collusion would be much frowned upon but in 1981 it was quite commonplace. Indeed the head groundsman at Hove, Peter Eaton, had become one of my closest allies as we tried to baffle our opponents. As often as not we were too clever for our own good and our strategy would backfire on us.

The reason for our choice of pitch at Eastbourne was, quite simply, Derek Underwood. For many years, he had been the scourge of Sussex and many other teams, particularly on rain-affected or dry pitches on which he could be lethal.

*

Ever since I first came across Underwood, at Hastings in 1973, it had been my determined mission to nip his deadly influence in the bud and bring him down to the level of a normal spinner. In that encounter, our first match of the season and one of the first of my career, Kent scored 282 in their first innings, the highlight of which was the innings of Colin Cowdrey. Polite and courteous as ever, when he had scored just 18 he clipped a gentle legside half-volley from my bowling in the air straight to Tony Greig at mid-wicket and became my second first-class victim. At lunch, he shook me warmly by the hand and said, "Well bowled." I liked that.

The next day, a very wet morning followed by bright sunshine, provided the perfect conditions for the Kent bowlers to exploit, and Sussex were shot out for 67 by Graham and Underwood. I made nought, caught at slip by Cowdrey off Underwood. Colossal thunderstorms overnight then flooded the ground completely, and it seemed that Sussex might be spared a second innings. But the Kent players took it upon themselves to roll up their trousers and paddle about barefoot, helping the Sussex fire brigade to pump gallons of water off the ground and so mop up the sodden outfield. The Sussex team sat by gloomily watching these activities without so much as lifting a finger.

I was, of course, a distinctly interested party for I was on a pair and desperately worried that I might once again have to face Underwood in the second innings. I had been practising my forward defensive shot over and over again in the dressing room and was cursing the presence of the fire brigade and fervently praying that it would fail in its mission and that the match would be abandoned.

My prayers went unheeded. With two hours remaining, Underwood took the new ball and, by the time my turn came, we were 22 for five. I was trembling as Underwood ran in to bowl.

His first delivery was a faster ball, and to my surprise I middled it. But Luckhurst at short leg dived full length to prevent my escape to the other end so I was still stuck on my pair. The next ball was more viciously spun and, as I pushed forward, it reared up at me like a spitting cobra, struck me on the thumb and flew once again to Cowdrey at slip who gratefully swallowed the catch.

Caught Cowdrey, bowled Underwood for the second time in the match. The distinguished nature of the dismissals was my only consolation.

Underwood took eight for nine in ten overs, and we were all out for 54.

*

Sussex have suffered many times at the hands of Underwood since then but never so dramatically as this. It had always been my burning desire to snuff out his demonic powers, and the grassy pitch at Eastbourne was perhaps my chance. It was a sort of latter-day body-line tactic aimed at reducing the potency of a freakish and brilliant performer.

As luck would have it, I lost the toss and it was Sussex that had to bat first on a pitch that was barely distinguishable from the rest of the square and outfield. It served us right, I suppose, but, as is so often the case, the surface did not play as badly as it looked, and Mendis and I shared in an opening partnership of 114 before Mendis departed and I was joined by Booth-Jones.

After some excellent innings early in the summer, Booth-Jones was now having a wretched time with the bat. He was playing so badly, in his opinion, that he felt he would hardly now have justified a place in Hastings' second XI. His confidence was at an all-time low and, as if that were not enough, he was also being given a hard time by his two sisters, Caroline and Clare, who both had a serious crush on Imran and were desperate to meet him. With the season slipping away fast and Booth-Jones's place in the side becoming increasingly vulnerable, they were constantly pestering him to arrange for an introduction. The poor man, bullied in equal measure by bowlers on the field and sisters off it, was probably keen to have a break and a few days off by the seaside.

Booth-Jones never quite plucked up the courage to organise a meeting, and so the girls had to make do with trudging off to the club shop where signed photographs were on sale – except, in the case of Imran, they weren't. Sold out. "We've got plenty of Booth-Joneses," they were told, but that was not what they wanted at all.

As for Tim, nothing was going right. He soon played down the wrong line to a straight ball from Kevin Jarvis and was bowled.

This brought Parker in to join me. He was a completely different kettle of fish. Bristling with confidence and oozing with runs, he was challenging for a place in the Test side. But, before he had even faced a ball, disaster struck.

I played a ball to Chris Cowdrey fielding at mid-wicket and, in my enthusiasm, became confused and said "yes" instead of "no". Parker set off obediently but I, realising my error, abruptly sent him back. By then, he was too far committed, slipped and tried to scramble back on all fours, ending up grovelling flat out on his front with his arm outstretched and bat reaching forlornly for the crease. The bowler, Bob Woolmer, grabbed the ball, broke the wicket and appealed. The umpire, Derek Shackleton, looked at Parker sadly and said, "I'm very sorry, Paul, but I'm afraid I'm going to have to give you out." Greig came in instead and proceeded to hit six crisp boundaries; it was some time before we risked another single.

At least Underwood didn't take any wickets, and the stage was now set for our seamers. Things could not have gone much better. Kent barely managed 100 in their first innings and, following on, were dismissed for 254. Only Cowdrey and Tavaré showed much resistance and we were left with just 50 runs to win, which we achieved with little bother – except for poor Booth-Jones, who failed once again.

That was the last we saw of Tim. He was much missed but it paved the way for the return to the side of Colin Wells.

Caroline and Clare never did get to meet Imran.

We had taken our revenge on Kent, but things didn't run all our way. In the Sunday competition, they beat us on a faster run rate, by one run, after some confusion about the rules, and that prevented us from going to the top of the table. As I drove home on Sunday evening, listening to *'Your Hundred Best Tunes'* with Alan Keith, I had to accept that the county championship was now the only realistic target left. We had lost too often on Sundays and were now out of contention.

*

Derbyshire were our second visitors to the Eastbourne cricket week. The weather had changed – it was now hot – and so had the pitch. Instead of the green surface that had been planned, the groundsman had had second thoughts and shorn off the grass. Not unreasonably he wanted to produce something that looked more like a real cricket pitch.

Indeed, the pitch proved to be as good-natured as it looked and, although I managed to sustain a nasty blow to my right thumb and had to retire hurt, batting came pretty easily to everyone else; so much so that by the last day, the match had reached something of a stalemate with Derbyshire seemingly happy to bat through to the close of play without thought of making a declaration and opening up the game.

We were now beginning to find out life was that much tougher at the top of the table and that we could expect no favours from anyone and we certainly weren't getting any.

It was mid-afternoon on the final day and David Steele was batting ponderously with Alan Hill. Both were determined not to get out and ensure they saved the match. Colin Wells, normally a medium-pacer, was bowling his leg-breaks, having earlier taken the wickets of Peter Kirsten, the fine South African batsman, and Geoff Miller. But Steele and Hill were blocking resolutely.

Hill had always been one of my favourite players. He had the gnarled and weather-beaten face of a man burdened by the worries and uncertainties of batting for a living. His stance had become as contorted as his face. He was hardly a pretty player but one whose style gave me great comfort for, in him, I had at last found a batsman whose rate of scoring runs was similar to mine. I was always sad to see him go, this time run out by Parker when attempting a quick single. Oppressed by the cares of the world, Hill dragged himself back to the pavilion.

Wells continued his spell to Steele who, undaunted by the run-out, maintained his staunch defiance, and to Kim Barnett, a useful young leg-spinner himself. After three successive maiden overs Imran, fielding in the deep at square leg and getting mightily bored beneath the giant Town Hall clock, which boomed out its chimes every quarter of an hour, came running over to me with an excited look in his eye.

"Johnny, I want to bowl," he said.

"You what?" I replied, rather taken aback.

"Yes, I want to bowl," Imran insisted. "Conditions are just right. I am going to put on my bowling boots," and so he ran off in the direction of the pavilion. When he was not bowling or didn't expect to bowl, Imran used to wear his rather unattractive and unwhitened trainers because they were more comfortable for his feet than his big bowling boots. He scampered off and, for the next over, we continued with ten men.

It was a rare and wonderful thing when, as captain, your fast bowler actually wanted to bowl and, irrespective of conditions, it was not an opportunity to be turned down lightly. Imran's intervention had been totally unexpected. It was a hot afternoon, a good batting pitch, an old ball and a long journey to Nottingham beckoning. The game appeared to be drifting peacefully to its conclusion.

Imran had other ideas.

"Give me the ball," he said, grabbing it and rubbing it gleefully in his hands. He had the remarkable ability to make the oldest and shabbiest ball shine like a pearl. "Perfect," he said as he marked out his run, and between us we set the field. "Start defensive," he said, "and then, when I'm ready, we attack." I wisely did as I was told, and out of the blue the game came alive.

"Come on, Fred," shouted Gould from behind the stumps. 'Fred' was the unlikely and in many ways unsuitable nickname for our somewhat aristocratic fast bowler. It was derived from Fred Karno's travelling circus and seemed to us to be as good a way as any to address Imran and bring him down to earth a bit at the same time.

Imran grinned and began his spell. Nothing happened for a while, but Imran persevered with the circus tent behind him while Wells continued to lob up his leg-breaks, only occasionally pitching them, from the other end. The batsmen were both watchful and respectful.

Deadlock. For a moment I had the ball in my hands and was about to throw it back to Imran again for him to bowl his next over when I had a bright idea.

"This ball is in a terrible mess," I said. "It looks as though it's been chewed by a dog. Why don't we try and get it changed for a better one?"

"No, no," shouted Imran. "This ball is perfect for my requirements. You still do not understand the finer points of fast bowling."

"Fair enough," I said and jogged back to my position at slip, sorry that I wouldn't have the chance to complain about the ball to the umpires. I had seen other captains do it successfully. It had become rather a fashionable thing to do.

Imran continued to bowl. "He's beginning to swing it, skip," Gould whispered to me. No one then knew anything about reverse swing, but that is exactly what was happening. There was hope, but not much time left. Then Waller, who had taken over from Wells, bowled Barnett at the other end. That opened up the game, and we were now taking things very seriously.

Imran immediately trapped Steele lbw and, a man inspired, proceeded to wipe out the rest of their batting. Four wickets fell in five balls, all bowled or lbw. The batsmen were baffled by late swing at high pace. Rarely have I ever seen such a devastating spell of bowling with an old ball.

Imran, not surprisingly, was well pleased with himself. "That was clever bowling," he said as we all left the field. "Now I want to bat."

"Oh, that's good," I said.

"I want to bat high in the order. I feel it is my day and we must now beat this lot. I shall bat at four," he said. "The others won't mind."

I couldn't help but feel that such commitment from Imran was a good thing and to be encouraged. So he, who, for some reason, had batted at seven in the first innings, was promoted to number four on this whim and the rest of the order was reshuffled accordingly.

"Why do you always let him have his own way?" someone asked me.

"Because he says he's going to win the match for us," I answered and left it at that.

Sussex needed 234 runs to win in roughly 40 overs. It wasn't quite Tunbridge Wells again, but six an over was still a tall order. Mendis was out early, but Gould and Parker gave us a good start before Gould, after three cracking fours, was caught on the boundary. Parker made a few more runs before he, too, succumbed. He, as far as I can remember, then headed straight to the bar and, steadily becoming merrier, watched the spectacle unfold. With my injured thumb I, too, was reduced to spectating.

Imran, as ever adorned with his floppy hat, entered the stage and began to set about Derbyshire's bowling. He batted like a man with a mission, hit three sixes and eleven fours and laid waste all that Derbyshire set before him. His hundred that afternoon was one of his greatest innings.

A record crowd – 25,000 people came to Eastbourne that week – was ecstatic. It was thrilling stuff. Imran swept Derbyshire aside, and Sussex won in spectacular style with five balls to spare.

Imran's batting performance was perhaps reminiscent of Ted Dexter at his imperious best, so precisely and dominantly did he play.

Ian Botham was not the only all-rounder in the country capable of winning matches single-handed.

*

Eastbourne had always been a favourite ground for Imran. The pitch, low and flat, was ideal for his swing bowling and, for the same reason, also suited his batting. Two years later he made another glorious hundred at the Saffrons, this time watched by his girlfriend of the time, Emma. Not actually watched, in fact, because she, being a very fine artist, spent the day behind the hospitality tents painting a view of the ground.

After Imran was out, he strolled round to see her and found me there chatting about her work.

She looked up. "Hi there," she said. "What have you been up to?"

"Haven't you been watching?" Imran replied. "I've been scoring a hundred."

"Oh how marvellous," she went on. "And what do you think of my picture?"

Not only was Emma very talented but she was also very good for Imran, having absolutely no interest in cricket. She never watched a ball if she could possibly help it.

Later that year, I visited an exhibition of her paintings at Agnews in London. Most of them were of Imran draped about in her flat looking glamorous, but there was just one little pencil drawing that was also of interest to me – an old man asleep on a bench.

"Who's this?" I asked.

"Oh, that one," she said. "I did that at Hove. You can have it if you like."

"Can I really?"

"Yes." She took it off the wall, turned it over and wrote on the back, 'Old man watching you bat at Hove, with love from Emma.' I was rather touched.

So she knew a bit more about cricket than she made out.

*

Our victory over Derbyshire elevated us to second place in the table, now just four points behind Nottinghamshire, who were our next opponents. We had put behind us the disappointments of Guildford and Leicester, and our confidence was restored. We were back in the saddle.

But, as always, there wasn't much time in which to celebrate our victory. Just a quick slosh in the big bath and then off to Nottingham, after struggling through Eastbourne's Friday night holiday traffic.

For some reason that I now can't remember I was travelling with Imran, the hero of the moment. He eased into the passenger seat and made himself as comfortable as possible as we embarked upon our journey. First stop, London.

Before settling down to listen to *'Pick of the Week'* and *'Any Questions'*, we tuned into the sports desk which gave us the latest news from the fifth Test match at Old Trafford, now at the end of its second day. Amidst all the excitement at Eastbourne and Imran's astonishing exploits, the Test match had rather slipped our mind. It was reassuring to hear Brian Johnston's fruity voice – full of good cheer – summarising the day's play.

It had been a good one for England for whom Allott, playing in his first Test match on his home ground, and Willis added 56 priceless runs to the previous overnight score of 175 for nine. A final total of 231 was surely still well short of Brearley's expectations but, when Australia dramatically collapsed on the second afternoon for just 130, the Ashes seemed to be in the bag. It had been a marvellous day for both Sussex and England.

At least it had been until we joined the nose-to-tail, bumper-to-bumper queue of holiday traffic heading out of Eastbourne. The cars were filled with hot and tired passengers, making their way home from the seaside with its funfairs and bandstands, from the tennis at Devonshire Park, and even maybe from the cricket. It was a mass exodus, and the A22 could not cope.

"Oh God, we shall never get to Nottingham tonight," Imran remarked as he closed his eyes and stretched himself out. "We are not even moving."

He was very perceptive. We had come to a complete and seemingly permanent halt outside Polegate. Eventually we got going but it took an eternity to reach London, and that wasn't even half way there.

I didn't often travel with Imran, but he was the most undemanding of passengers. He slept all the way to London, where we stopped for a bite to eat, and thereafter to Nottingham. There was plenty of time for reflection as we plodded on up the motorway heading north and this I did on my own when I should, I suppose, have been chewing over my tactics with Imran for the big match ahead and pondering the likes of Rice and Hadlee, Randall, Hemmings and the pitch, of course.

Instead, the presence of Imran in the car reminded me of the one and only time we had ever shared a room together. It was in Derby the night before a Sunday League match in 1979. Those were the days long before either of us was entitled to a single room. We were then junior players.

We arrived at our hotel late and tired. I was sitting in bed reading a book and generally unwinding from the journey when Imran, wide awake and bored, switched on the television.

"Ah good, a film," he said, settling himself down to watch.

"Great," I said, trying to show some enthusiasm while inwardly despairing at the prospect. "What's the film?"

"*Marathon Man*," answered Imran and made himself a cup of tea as the grisly plot began to unfold.

For those who have not seen the film, I won't go into the details except to say that it is a gripping tale of unimaginable tension which reaches a climax of ghastliness when Dustin Hoffman is seated in a dentist's chair having a tooth extracted without anaesthetic by Laurence Olivier. Olivier is playing a malevolent torturer, who has in his past operated upon Jews in the Nazi concentration camps.

After two hours of relentless misery and discomfort, I was hiding beneath the blankets. Worse still, I was wide awake. Imran simply turned over at the end of the film and fell asleep whilst I lay in bed until I could bear it no longer. At first light, I got up, dressed and went for a walk round Derby where, at least, I found some peace and quiet on the Sunday morning.

Imran and I decided thereafter that we were incompatible room mates and so never shared again.

*

As we finally reached Nottingham at two in the morning, my bed – in a single room – had never seemed so welcome.

CHAMPIONSHIP TABLE – 14 AUGUST

		Played	Points
1.	Nottinghamshire	17	208
2.	Sussex	17	204
3.	Essex	16	187
4.	Surrey	17	173

Chris Waller

Chapter Thirteen
Clash of the Titans

v Nottinghamshire: at Trent Bridge, August 15,17,18

In 1981 *Wisden* listed the champion county for every summer since 1864 and, of all those who had played in the early years, the name of Sussex did not appear amongst the winners. It was a state of affairs I was determined to put right.

From those February days watching the sun set over Coogee Bay in Australia to pre-season strategy sessions, motorways, dressing rooms – and, of course, the cricket – my whole year had been devoted to this one cause.

We were a happy team and had pulled together, so much so that we were fielding almost identical sides from match to match. Booth-Jones may have lost his place, but he had played an important role and even Imran's injury, which could have knocked us back a bit, came at a fortunate time, when the cricket calendar was not quite so frantic.

Yet I knew, as we all did, that this match at Trent Bridge was the big one. We had to beat Nottinghamshire, not just to take us to the top of the table but to leave us perfectly placed for the final furlong of the championship.

It was 'The Clash of the Titans', which appropriately enough was showing in the local cinema at the time.

Clive Rice, the Nottinghamshire captain, would have felt exactly the same. Notts had, at least, won the championship before – but not since 1929. He was as desperate to win it as I was.

Both teams had won their previous two matches but Nottinghamshire had one huge advantage. They were playing at home and, more pertinent still, there was the much talked about Trent Bridge pitch. All summer this had been the source of great speculation, and I was as intrigued as anyone to see what they would prepare for us.

I was not unduly surprised by what I found. The pitch had been used before, frequently probably. It was still quite green down the middle but brown and worn at one end. The other end showed a different shade of green and texture, and closer inspection confirmed that this had been brought about by a sprinkling of grass cuttings rolled into the surface. It was a clever piece of camouflage designed, I assume, to make you think it was green and grassy when it wasn't. Beneath the grass the pitch was as rough as it was at the other end. Ron Allsop, the groundsman, was a cunning operator. "A clever trick," Imran would say.

It was useful intelligence, but didn't clear my mind for the possibility of winning the toss. Chasing a fourth innings target on such a pitch would in all likelihood be very troublesome. Batting first would also have its perils, as most counties had already discovered. All of them had batted first, and not one of them had yet passed 200.

Rice, for whom I had great admiration, had devised a highly effective winning formula, based upon the fast bowling of Richard Hadlee and himself and supported by the increasingly effective off-spin of Eddie Hemmings – on wickets that played to those strengths. Hemmings, particularly, was having an astonishingly successful year, exploiting the bounce and turn of the Trent Bridge square upon which I had always enjoyed bowling myself.

Despite all this, even Rice seemed at something of a loss when he won the toss. In April Bucks Fizz had won the Eurovision song contest with a catchy little tune called *'Making Your Mind Up'*, which Rice might well have had on the brain as he wrestled with the torment that comes with indecision.

The strength of the Sussex batting might have given him pause for thought. Mendis, Parker, Imran and Greig were all in top form and yet, predictably in the end, he stuck to his trusted formula and asked us to bat first.

My two favourite pursuits in life were fishing and cricket, and I had often noticed that they had one thing in common. Fishing for me has consisted mostly in not catching fish and cricket largely in not scoring runs. Failure had been an almost constant feature and the ensuing challenge all the more enticing for it.

This day began like many others. Early on, I got a nasty, leaping ball from Rice, which I could only spoon to the gully fieldsman before retiring disconsolately to the pavilion, where I watched

Mendis and Parker coolly steer us into calmer waters. They were still together at lunch by which time Sussex had built the foundations for an imposing total.

It was not to be. Soon after lunch disaster struck. Parker clipped a ball to mid-on and set off for a run but, by the time Mendis had convinced him he was staying put, Parker was too far committed, even for one so agile, and was despairingly run out. Imran, now promoted to number four after his heroics at Eastbourne, celebrated his elevation in the batting order by hoisting Hemmings for two fours and a mighty six into the pavilion before chancing his arm once too often and slicing a high catch to Hadlee at cover. It was dazzling cricket but not quite what was wanted.

Hemmings, having withstood this early buffeting, now got into his stride on a pitch already taking spin, and he quietly squeezed the life out of the Sussex batting like a giant boa constrictor while one after another we flailed about in the grip of his powerful hold.

Our final score of 208 was a great disappointment after being at one time 105 for one, but at least it was the highest that summer by a team batting first at Nottingham. When Robinson and the fidgety Randall fell quickly before bad light stopped play, honours were just about even.

*

Meanwhile at Old Trafford, with England again on the ropes, Botham scored 118 in two hours of ferocious power and effortless stroke play. He fairly launched into Lillee, Alderman and Bright and his partnership of 149 with Tavaré, playing doggo at the other end, transformed the match and paved the way for Knott and Emburey to make half-centuries of their own. The outcome of all this was that Australia required the mammoth target of 506 runs to win the match.

I went to church on Sunday morning, but it seemed that not even the power of prayer could influence our waning fortunes in the Sunday League. Any hopes we may still have had of the title evaporated at the hands of Nottinghamshire, who beat us fair and square on a hot afternoon. No one distinguished themselves except for Imran who, in a last gasp effort, took five wickets but to no avail.

"If only I had more support, Johnny," he said to me afterwards with a forlorn look in his face.

At least I couldn't blame myself for this latest defeat as I didn't play. I had sustained an unusual leg injury while fielding during the last over of play on Saturday night. I was standing at slip when the batsman, Todd, edged a ball low to my right along the ground. I dived to stop it but, instead of grabbing the ball, I landed on it and bruised my thigh in the process. I suppose it could have been worse, but by Sunday morning I was hobbling about and ruled out of action.

*

The rest on Sunday did me a power of good, and by Monday morning I was fit enough to bowl the first over of the day to that great Nottinghamshire stalwart, Basharat Hassan. Full of hope I trotted in to bowl the first ball, and it was rather a good one. It landed right on a length and kicked a little as Hassan pushed tentatively forward and the ball struck the inside edge of his bat, hit his pad and lobbed gently into the hands of Paul Phillipson at short leg.

Almost simultaneously I heard a shout of "no ball" which echoed around the ground. I turned in disbelief to see Arthur Jepson, the umpire, signalling a no ball to the scorers. Hassan had been reprieved. It was, I think, the first and only no ball I ever bowled, and it cost us a vital wicket. Who would have believed it? In my eagerness I had taken my run-up from the wrong mark and paid a heavy price.

Hassan went on from this early slice of luck to complete a belligerent half-century – while all around him wickets fell. Waller who was proving every bit as effective as Hemmings took five wickets. I, too, managed to pull myself together and take three. By soon after lunch Nottinghamshire had meekly surrendered for 102, with Hassan left not out on 58. So we prepared to bat for a second time with an impressive lead of 106.

*

At Old Trafford it was an altogether different game, with the pitch easing all the time. Australia, after a poor start, were making a spirited attempt to reach their huge target. Yallop and Border both made hundreds; the score crept past 300, and it did seem just conceivable that Australia might produce yet another twist in this extraordinary series.

But it didn't last. Willis, Allott, Emburey and, of course, Botham shared the wickets and England won the match by 103 runs and so clinched one of the most remarkable series in Test history to retain the Ashes.

*

Back at Nottingham the cricket was no less tense. Rice this time opened the bowling with spin, and before we knew it we were in deep trouble at 37 for five. The batsmen froze, and the atmosphere in the dressing room became cold and clammy. All of a sudden it was Nottinghamshire on the rampage, and our first championship title was slipping away. Greig and Gould led a partial recovery but, by the end of the day, we had been bowled out for 144, setting Nottinghamshire a target of 251 to win.

Sleep would have come easily to neither set of players that night.

Trent Bridge is one of the country's more intimate and comfortable cricket grounds, surrounded on two sides by unpretentious two-tier terraced seating that amply accommodates the locals. The pavilion, although on a grander scale, is more akin to a country house, as compared with the stately homes of Lord's and the Oval, and beautifully adorned with window boxes, filled with petunias and geraniums.

The spectators, fiercely partisan and sometimes vociferous, give the ground its spirit and atmosphere. There was often a group of them bunched close together on the top tier of the stand more or less behind, or rather above, the sightscreen at the Radcliffe Road end, opposite the pavilion. They were prone to give the home team as much grief as their opponents.

The final morning began with a string of maidens which put everyone's nerves on edge until eventually in the eleventh over Imran found the edge of Todd's bat and Gould took a good catch. Six for one was the meagre score as Randall strolled jauntily into bat singing to himself.

"Show them the way, Coco," shouted a voice from behind the sightscreen, using one of Randall's many nicknames and attributed to the famous circus clown.

"I'll try, I'll try," Randall shouted back.

He took guard, banging his Gunn and Moore bat fiercely into the popping crease and wandered about talking to himself and to anyone near him who would listen. While being quite mad in the most lovable way, Randall was also a very good batsman. He had made a real name for himself in cricketing history by scoring an outstanding century in the Centenary Test match at Melbourne in 1977.

"Come on Rags, come on Rags, you can do it," (that was another nickname) he repeated to himself loudly as Imran ran in to bowl. First ball, Imran fizzed one down at him with vicious speed, just clipping Randall's glove on the way through to Gould behind the wicket.

"Unlucky, Rags, unlucky," Randall murmured as he whistled his way back to the pavilion. Six for two. Back in came the redoubtable Hassan who had played so well in the first innings.

While Randall was a great Trent Bridge favourite, Hassan had, over the years, been given a hard time by the Radcliffe Road end barrackers for slow scoring. He wasn't the only one. Mike Smedley in the 1970s had also been a target and 'Knocker' White, now a first-class umpire, used to take some flak, too. Earlier still, Brian Bolus got his fair share of abuse, but he could give as good as he got. In those days there would have been a lively exchange of words.

But 'Basher' was in good form and so back in their good books. It was he and Robinson who carefully repaired the damage and survived until lunch, by which time the score had trickled on to 71 for two. It had been a tense and tortuous morning.

Immediately after lunch I got a ball to bounce and turn at Robinson. And it lobbed up off his glove and gave Gould time to nip round from behind the stumps, dive into the dust in front of the hapless batsman and make the catch.

73 for three and Rice marched to the crease, upright as a soldier, to join Hassan who was holding the innings together. Gradually, throughout the afternoon, these two took control. We tried spin and pace but all to no avail as Nottinghamshire caught a scent of victory.

Hitherto, the weather had been fine, if a bit humid. Bare torsos in the crowd had been exposed to the sun, balding heads protected by floppy hats or handkerchiefs knotted at the corners. It was a typical high summer scene in the Midlands.

But, as the afternoon wore on, the weather became sultry and heavy. Clouds bubbled up from nowhere and smothered the sun. The light began to fade. A glimmer of hope for Sussex emerged from the encroaching gloom. I reasoned that our fast bowlers would be a tough proposition in such conditions but that neither Rice nor Hassan would wish to go off if offered the light.

I deliberately slowed down the tempo of the game both to increase the drama and to play upon the batsmen's nerves. In the Stygian gloom, Imran and le Roux proceeded to bowl very fast and with great hostility, and gradually the batsmen lost their momentum.

The crowd didn't like it, either – or, to be more accurate, didn't like me.

"Get on with it, Barclay," they shouted aggressively. "Why don't you go and work in Woolworth's if you're going to take so much time?"

In a way it was flattering to be the focus of so much attention. The outcome was that I placed the field with increasingly meticulous precision. Rather childishly, I couldn't resist baiting the crowd. The umpires then offered the batsmen the light but, not surprisingly, they turned it down. Progress was agonisingly slow.

By tea, Notts had crept on to 144 for three. We just couldn't make the breakthrough. Equally, I felt that they were going to find it difficult to score 107 in the final session in these conditions.

By now a large crowd had built up all round the ground. News must have got about that this match was reaching a dramatic climax. For those arriving immediately after tea, Imran was still steaming in from the Radcliffe Road end while I was wheeling away from the Pavilion end. I liked bowling in tandem with Imran and always felt it gave me a better chance, batsmen being so relieved to get away from Imran's end that they might drop their guard and concentration when facing me.

At long last we struck. Hassan, after batting stoically for more than three and a half hours, was bowled by Imran for 79. It had been as if we were fishing for a whole afternoon in barren waters, just as those patient fishermen do every weekend on the River Trent without a bite for ages, not since Robinson, in fact – but now we had drawn a big fish into the net. "Where there is one, there could always be more," I told myself. We still had a chance.

Hadlee joined Rice with the score 174 for four and promptly lofted me over mid-off for six. The light was still gloomy but not as dark as before. The crowd was noisy, hot and bothered. They cheered every run ecstatically. Rice, far from his usual confidant and dominant self, was beginning to prod nervously until, in the end, he tamely spooned up a catch to Arnold at mid-wicket. 188 for five, and 63 more runs needed.

Five runs later the spectators were stunned into silence when Hadlee tried to hit me again for six but, instead, hoiked up a high swirling catch to Arnold again, this time at mid-off, which he held without fuss.

"Never in doubt," he said, as he clasped the ball to his chest and then looked at the scoreboard. 193 for six. "It's a bit of a teaser now, isn't it?"

For the first time in the day Nottinghamshire were beginning to look shaky.

Le Roux now returned to the attack and began to bowl very fast. Birch and French managed a few singles, between them but they were unconvincing and it was no surprise when le Roux ripped one through French's defence to have him well caught by Gould. The score was now 205 for seven and Notts 46 runs short of their target.

Hemmings made his way slowly to the crease. He looked around the field and then at the scoreboard, which now made uncomfortable reading for the home team, and finally up at the sky as though seeking divine inspiration. A Notts victory was now all but out of the question.

The crowd had changed its tune, too, for, having cheered every run with frenzied enthusiasm for most of the day, it was now faced with the prospect of a Sussex win. The shouts of "What about the over rate?" had changed to "What about the light?"

'Lead kindly light amidst the encircling gloom,' the famous hymn tells us. Neither Hemmings nor Birch wanted to be led anywhere other than to the sanctuary of the pavilion. With fifteen overs of the final twenty remaining, and the crowd in uproar, the umpires were impelled to bring the players off because of gloomy light.

During the break I tried to persuade the umpires that the light was no worse than when it had originally been offered to Rice and Hassan.

They at least listened to me and, after the loss of seven precious overs, relented, and we returned to the field and continued the battle.

Birch did not last long after the resumption and fell lbw to le Roux who then bowled Cooper first ball. 210 for nine, and Nottinghamshire were clinging on for dear life.

Mike Bore came in at number eleven. A capable left-arm bowler, he had a batting record of marked indistinction, being quite unscathed by natural ability in this department. He looked ill at ease and wore a white motor cycle crash helmet to protect his head as he prepared to face two of the world's best and fastest bowlers.

Imran behaved like a bull, pawing the ground, itching to get at the batsmen. Le Roux was more controlled – but still a tough proposition in the fading light, with nine men surrounding the bat.

I could see the Notts team clustered together in their dressing room, with strict instructions not to move from where they were seated. Even Randall had to sit still.

Their hopes rested on the last pair, every ball an ordeal in itself. Bore and Hemmings rarely made contact but so long as they survived the raucous Nottinghamshire crowd let out a huge cheer. Bore needed all the encouragement he could get.

Imran turned at the end of his run-up and prepared to bowl again to the ill-equipped Bore. Legs pumping and arms rolling, a touch of Michael Holding in his style, he accelerated towards the crease. There was complete hush around the ground as he released the ball at lethal speed.

Bore plainly never saw it, but instinctively he went back towards his stumps and the ball hit him on the shin of his back leg very hard and with a loud thwack.

The whole of the Sussex team, now gathered in a wide arc behind the stumps, exploded in appeal. All the energy and excitement, the triumphs and the upsets, the sheer euphoria of that thrilling summer burst forth in that moment.

The crowd drew in a breath; the Notts players sat stock still on the balcony, and all eyes turned upon the hapless umpire, Peter Stevens. Ever since Tunbridge Wells we had, a little unkindly I thought, prefixed his name with 'Shaking'.

Time stood still.

He deliberated long and hard, digested all the evidence, then shook his head.

"Not out," he said.

The crowd roared its approval, releasing its venom upon the Sussex fielders.

Was it out? We, of course, all thought so. Both wicket-keeper and bowler thought it was plumb. There was not even the possibility that it had hit Bore's bat, which was about as much use as a stick of celery. The only explanation was that the ball just might have been drifting down the leg-side.

In the remaining few balls we continued to throw everything we had at Bore and Hemmings, but the moment had passed and victory had eluded our grasp.

Whatever else, it had been a magnificent game of cricket. At the press conference afterwards Rice admitted, "It was the tensest draw I have ever played in."

For three whole days we had all been governed by nerve-racking tension, made worse by the snail's-pace tempo of the match. It was like a game of chess in which both sides had slowly tried to force an opening. The balance had tilted this way and that, yet the result in the end was a stalemate. Championship cricket.

Yet the day's drama was not over. The mood of the crowd, especially those in the pavilion, was hostile. Despite Nottinghamshire's heroic survival, it seemed that we had not been forgiven for slowing the game down earlier in the day.

"Come on, let's all go up the steps together into the pavilion," I said as we left the field, sensing that this was a moment for solidarity. I stuck close to Arnold and le Roux, whom I thought looked big enough and brave enough to master any crisis and lend me support.

It didn't really help for as I was nearing the top of the steps, I was suddenly grabbed by the shirt and hauled across the seats by a large woman who, I couldn't help noticing, had terrible gaps in her teeth. She proceeded to shout obscenities at me, nearly drowning me with spit. I had never been assaulted before, let alone by a woman, and, when eventually she released her grip, I found myself wondering what Ian Botham might have done in the same circumstances. It was a pleasing link with the great man if nothing else.

Back in the sanctuary of the dressing room, Imran was inconsolable.

"Plumb, it was absolutely plumb," he kept groaning. "That Shakin' chap must be blind."

Champagne was being opened, the legacy of a *Sunday Telegraph* team of the month award. We had been carrying it around with us for ages and now seemed as good a time as any to drink it both to drown out our disappointment and celebrate a great match.

"Home crowd, I suppose," bellowed Gould, who was standing on a chair, determined not to waste any of the bubbly.

We all drank the champagne, all except Imran.

"It was plumb," he continued to complain.

*

Later the press challenged me about some of the more competitive phases of the game.

"There's £12,000 at stake for winning the championship," I said. "It was like a Test match out there, not a cocktail party, and obviously we were keen to win."

I don't know quite why I put it like that. It wasn't really what I was feeling at all. The money was absolutely secondary in my mind.

*

Eventually the dressing room quietened down. We packed up our cases and headed for home. Whatever the result, it had been a fine game and worthy of the two clubs fighting it out for the county championship.

With four matches each to play, the gap between us was now just two points.

CHAMPIONSHIP TABLE – 18 AUGUST

		Played	*Points*
1.	Nottinghamshire	18	212
2.	Sussex	18	210
3.	Surrey	18	196
4.	Essex	17	193

Ian Greig

Chapter Fourteen
Hot and Waspy

v Hampshire: at Bournemouth, August 26,27,28

It was a hot night as I drove back down the motorway from Nottingham alone, bound for my sister's house in London where I planned to stay the night and break the journey home. It was beginning to get darker in the evenings now, and I was confronted by a steady stream of traffic, headlights shining brightly, as I travelled south and reflected upon the events of the day.

It was Tuesday night, and we had three days off. Then on Saturday the now beleaguered Australians were visiting Hove for their last match before the final Test at The Oval.

I was fast running out of energy so my first stop on the journey was at Watford Gap service station, where I was faced by another world of passion and enthusiasm. The season's first football supporters were creating a rumpus outside the Burger King, where I bought a can of coke and a packet of crisps to ease my hunger and thirst. The events at Nottingham, I thought, wouldn't mean much to them, county cricket being a small world bound up in its own importance. Football would always take precedence over this.

The timing of the Australian visit could have been better, coming as it did when the county season was reaching its climax and at the end of their tour when the series had already been decided. Both Sussex and Australian teams were exhausted and so there was great potential for grumpiness on all sides.

"Will you promise me one thing, Johnny?" Imran had said to me as he walked back to bowl on that final afternoon at Trent Bridge. "That I won't have to play against Australia."

In a decisive moment I gave him my word. After all, in the circumstances, it was a very reasonable request.

My problem was that I had very much set my heart upon winning the championship; the players all needed a rest and I certainly wasn't prepared to let the Australian match stand in my way.

But for all that the visit of the Australians was still a prestigious event and one much looked forward to by the members and public, the committee and sponsors. I had been put in a difficult position and would clearly never be able to keep everyone happy. In the end I didn't try to. After all, Sussex had never won the county championship before and would probably only rarely again have a better chance than this. So I decided to pursue my ultimate goal with a single-mindedness not normally associated with Sussex cricket.

We fielded a weakened team against the Australians. Paul Parker was captain instead of me while Imran, Gould, le Roux, Waller and Arnold were all given the match off. I was roundly criticised. The sponsors weren't happy either and we lost a lot of friends, I was later told.

I suppose there was no right or wrong. The decision depended upon values and priorities. My hell-bent desire to win the championship was not shared by as many as I thought. I suspect that is the main reason why Sussex, in all its history, has never won this coveted prize. Hearts, as compared with those elsewhere, have never really been in it – as if there were something almost vulgar about winning; it was something that other people did. Perhaps not quite winning has always been part of the charm of Sussex cricket. Values are rather different in the South where appearances, rather than results, matter more than they do up North or in the Midlands.

As it turned out, our second-string team did not perform too badly. Both Jerry Heath and Tim Head scored fifties, and the Australians did not win the match until the final afternoon.

*

Meanwhile Nottinghamshire were in Birmingham, bowling Warwickshire out for 49 and winning with a day to spare. The gap in the championship table grew to 26 points even though we had a game in hand.

For our next match we travelled to Dean Park in Bournemouth, a ground surrounded by red-tiled villas and fir trees. The pavilion resembled a large holiday house in which Hampshire occupied the front room looking out over the ground while Sussex, as the visiting side, took over the servants' quarters at the back, all cramped with a splintery floor, bits of which would find their way into clothes and especially socks.

It was a hot and waspy match. The picnickers surrounding the boundary were plagued by the pestering insects and flapped at them to little avail.

Dean Park was apparently well known for its wasps. Legend has it that Hubert Doggart, captaining Sussex in the mid-1950s, swallowed one whilst fielding and had to be rushed to hospital.

In the dressing room le Roux became our champion swatter, lining up the corpses proudly on the window sill.

"Garth, you are so unkind," Imran said from his corner as – whack – another wasp met its end. Mercifully, no one got stung.

Bournemouth in August is a holiday resort with shops and children, sea and sand and all the ingredients of fun. For family holidays we used to visit Studland Bay around the other side of Poole harbour, and there we would make enormous sand castles built to resist the onslaught of the incoming tide – until they were finally bashed down by the force of nature.

"You can't hit against the tide," coaches would always tell us. "You must go with the flow and ease the ball away to where it wants to be hit."

In Sussex's first innings I tried to flick an away swinger through mid-wicket and was smartly snapped up by Gordon Greenidge at second slip. The tide had made its point.

But it was Hampshire who batted first and we were confident we could bowl them out twice and chase a target. The square at Bournemouth takes a little time to get used to, as it lies on a kind of plateau onto which bowlers have to run uphill from both ends. For a while neither Imran nor le Roux wanted to bowl from either end until eventually they took it in turns from the South, with a light breeze behind them.

To lift our hearts, after three belligerent fours, Greenidge – always a danger-man – was bowled by le Roux. From the pavilion in his place came a young player with just a hint of swagger and wearing a large, flamboyant sun hat. Mark Nicholas.

"Look, Garth, no helmet," Imran shouted over to le Roux.

Le Roux waved his hand in acknowledgement and proceeded to fizz the ball past Nicholas's nose to such an extent that he must have been relieved to get down to Arnold's end, where he could play an orthodox game and push forward more circumspectly. He was immediately caught at second slip, doing just that.

Hampshire folded up quite obligingly despite an innings of 32 from Tim Tremlett, which lasted nearly four hours. That was bad enough but, in glancing a ball from Imran down to fine leg, he forced le Roux to stub his left thumb into the ground and wince in agony. He made a lot of fuss at the time and later an x-ray revealed that he had actually broken it. Normally such an event in August would delight a county cricketer – the potential of two or three weeks off games.

"I've broken my thumb," he said sadly on his return from hospital.

"Oh dear," I replied. "I'm afraid broken thumbs don't count at this stage. You'll just have to strap it up, bite the bullet and get on with it."

Le Roux, who may have had visions of a few extra days' fishing, accepted his fate and grumpily settled down to watch us bat.

Imran followed up his four first innings wickets with a dazzling hundred and this made up for the absence of Paul Parker, who was making his debut for England in the final Test match at The Oval.

For Paul, it was to be his one and only opportunity. He could not have deserved his call-up more, batting brilliantly throughout the summer. He was also by far and away the best all-round fielder in the country – magnificent in the covers – fast, alert, athletic, and also he held some stinging catches in the slips and gully.

An eventful first day was almost complete when Gould's head was sent spinning by a sharp blow on the helmet from a ball bowled by Malcolm Marshall. The swelling was so intense and instantaneous that it proved quite impossible for a while to remove his helmet and attend to the wound. Broken thumbs and cracked heads were a menace, but injury had to be taken in its stride and eventually we got the helmet off.

Gould was in belting form again the next morning despite his headache. He made 35 not out, and with a lead of 89 in the first innings we were well on our way to victory. Our seamers then bowled out Hampshire for 223, and we won on the final day with eight wickets in hand.

Nottinghamshire, meanwhile, had won in two days at Cleethorpes and were still 28 points clear, but with our final three fixtures all at Hove we remained firmly in the hunt and full of hope.

CHAMPIONSHIP TABLE – 28 AUGUST

		Played	Points
1.	Nottinghamshire	20	260
2.	Sussex	19	232
3.	Essex	19	222
4.	Somerset	18	209

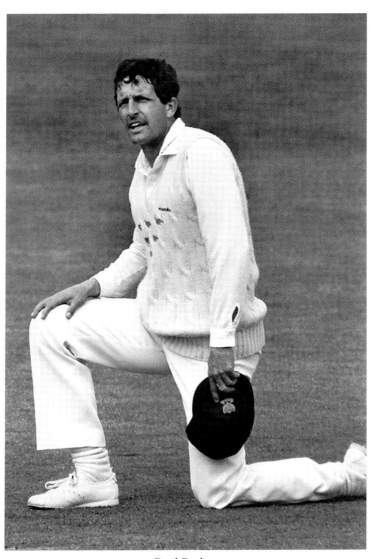

Paul Parker

Chapter Fifteen
Just Too Shy

v Middlesex: at Hove, August 29,31, September 1
v Hampshire: at Hove, September 2,3,4
v Yorkshire: at Hove, September 12,14,15

We needed one last burst of energy to carry us through the three remaining fixtures. The first was against Middlesex. The Test match had deprived us of Parker, but Middlesex themselves were missing Brearley, Gatting and Emburey. Added to which, we had a stroke of luck when Daniel strained his back after just four overs and was unable to bowl any more.

Daniel had always liked bowling at Hove. Many of us remembered only too well the battering we took in a Benson and Hedges match in 1978. On a grey day with the pitch very grassy he raced down the hill and took six for 17 in nine overs. It was about the most explosive spell of fast bowling I had ever seen at Hove – or anywhere else for that matter. On every subsequent visit Daniel roared in like a man inspired and so none of the Sussex batsmen was sorry to see him slope off to the pavilion with his sweater slung limply over his shoulder.

As if to celebrate Middlesex's misfortune Gould conjured up a lavish stream of drives and pulls, to reach his fifty against his old county in under an hour and looked mighty happy about it too. He had been denied the chance to show his former colleagues what he could do at Lord's earlier in the season when it had never stopped raining. On that occasion, in a rash moment, he had teed up a golf ball just inside the large dressing-room window and belted it with an eight iron out over the ground where it landed with a squelch on the square, narrowly missing Mick Hunt, the head groundsman.

Gould's sense of mischief and adventure had been a tonic to Sussex cricket and stood us in good stead all season. Alan Ross in *The Times* wrote, 'Gould has the look and shape of a bale of straw but, when it comes to cricket, he dives around like a performing seal.' Indeed, in this match he took a clutch of brilliant catches.

Imran, le Roux, and Greig did most of the damage with Imran leading the way taking ten wickets in all. "That was so easy," he proclaimed in the dressing room afterwards. We polished them off by lunchtime on the third day.

Nottinghamshire, though, had unfortunately beaten Derbyshire just as convincingly, and the gap between us was still an intimidating 28 points. We now knew that we had to win our final two matches and rely upon Notts slipping up against lowly Glamorgan in their final fixture at Trent Bridge.

*

Our next match, our game in hand, was against Hampshire at Hove, and so we tried to emulate our rivals in Nottingham by preparing a grassy pitch.

Colin Wells confirmed his return to form with his first century of the season, and Greig thrilled us too with his maiden championship hundred and ten wickets in the match as well. Back in Coogee Bay, I had banked on two or three players improving during the course of the season. Greig had definitely done just that and, in doing so, had made a huge difference to our team.

Facing our first innings score of over 400, Hampshire were always struggling. Off the very first ball Greenidge pushed le Roux into the covers and called Tremlett for a quick single, only to see Parker – still smarting from his disappointment at the Oval – pick it up and throw the wicket down in one easy motion.

Hampshire followed on and, despite a hundred from John Rice, we were left with just 22 to win.

The gap in the table with just one match remaining, was four tantalising points.

*

So, as this extraordinary season reached its climax in mid-September, we had to rely upon Glamorgan, rooted as they were near the bottom of the championship table, to thwart the ambitions of Nottinghamshire.

It was a tall order and not one which Glamorgan were capable of carrying out. For the tenth successive time at home Rice won the toss – the odds against this are apparently 1,024 to one – and by lunchtime on the first day Glamorgan had been bowled out for 60. All we could really hope for now was rain at Trent Bridge.

But instead, it was raining at Hove, where Yorkshire were the visitors. The match was delayed for a while before Imran and le Roux did their best to make up for lost time by bowling as fast as anything we had seen all season. By the end of the first day Yorkshire had collapsed to 148 for nine with Lumb suffering a fractured hand and Moxon aggravating a nose injury.

Bairstow hung on bravely at the end with Paul Jarvis who, at the age of 16, was the youngest player ever to play for Yorkshire. His was a fearsome baptism, and he took one withering blow beneath the heart which both shocked and winded him. It had been a bruising day but, sadly for Sussex, matters were now out of our hands.

Nottinghamshire had all but won at Trent Bridge.

On Monday, the second day, rain continued to check our final bid for glory but in one last despairing effort, we raced to 250 in just 40 overs. Colin Wells made a sparkling 80, and Imran, Mendis and Gould all thrashed the Yorkshire bowling mercilessly.

It was early in the afternoon that the news came through from Trent Bridge that Nottinghamshire had beaten Glamorgan by ten wickets and so won the championship. Despite this disappointment, our three batting points guaranteed us second place and, though Yorkshire were far from beaten, we celebrated as soon as play finished on Monday evening.

It so happened that one of our greatest supporters that summer had been the Brighton and Hove Albion striker Michael Robinson, who subsequently moved on to Liverpool where his career really took off. So delighted was he with our performances all season that he dropped a case of champagne into the dressing room to show his appreciation.

With the rain now teeming down outside, Gould shouted, "Come on boys, let's open the bottles now and get stuck in."

The champagne flowed and several players, including me, were thrown into the big bath.

Some time later when darkness had fallen Greig, I think it was, suddenly said, "What about a team streak, a run round the ground, a few stretches, and a team warm-up."

The players needed little encouragement and in no time at all were stripping off their cricket clothes for this impromptu training session, quite naked and led by Arnold as usual. Off they went into the darkness and pouring rain for an erratic and wayward lap of honour around the ground. Only lmran and I failed to join in.

"This is beneath my dignity," lmran said. I was just too shy.

They somehow completed a circuit of the ground before gathering in a circle somewhere near the middle to do some exercises. It was only then that le Roux, Greig and Gould noticed the plastic groundsheet covers protecting the pitches from the rain.

It was le Roux who started the fun and went first. Taking his normal run-up he fairly tore down the hill and hurtled himself, bottom first, onto the covers and slid inelegantly but effectively, with legs splayed in the air, and with some speed, down the full length of the pitch and ended up on the grass at the other end. The rest of the team followed him and in no time at all Parker, Phillipson, Greig, Gould, Arnold, Wells, Waller and Adrian Jones were joining in the fun.

Despite the darkness, the white bodies showed up well amidst the gloom. I watched all this from the pavilion steps, somewhat embarrassed, but soon I noticed I wasn't the only one observing the team's display. I had spotted the silhouette of a committee member sitting in the committee room on his own.

It was the chairman. After watching the proceedings with interest for a short while, he opened his *Times* newspaper, raised it above the level of his eyes and solemnly immersed himself in world events while the team, for which he was responsible, frolicked playfully on the slithery groundsheets until bottoms became so sore that they had to call it a day.

It was still not late. They had only just returned to the dressing room for a well-earned bath when Stewart Storey, our coach, reminded us that we were expected at the Mayor of Hove's reception in half an hour where, regretfully, even more drink would be offered. A very quick sobering-up session was needed and, by the time we had climbed into our blazers and ties, we looked almost presentable.

It was one of those confused and disconcerting parties, in which the key participants could not really compete on equal terms. The Sussex players, far from sober and undeniably boisterous, were the life and soul of the party, an event otherwise attended by rather drab and dreary councillors.

Parker was not at his best. He tended to become a little argumentative and obstreperous after a few drinks. I watched him having a heated debate with the vicar of Hove. The longer the conversation progressed, I noticed, the more Parker's glass of beer began to tilt – until he was slopping his drink over the vicar's shoes. As I walked over to rescue the situation Parker, in a slurred voice, concluded their conversation by saying, "Quite frankly, vicar, I think you're talking complete shit." It was at this point that I decided we should say our goodbyes and bid the mayor and his party farewell.

*

Our behaviour may have been bad, but it was nothing compared with the visit of the 1972 Australians to Buckingham Palace. The Aussies had just completed an extraordinary victory at Lord's after Bob Massie had astonishingly taken 16 wickets in the match. On the Monday afternoon the Queen had been due to make her traditional visit to Lord's to meet the teams but, because of the early finish, plans were rearranged and instead, the Queen invited the Australian team back to the Palace for tea.

As you can imagine, before the Australians ever reached the palace, there had been some serious celebrations in the dressing room, where a mixture of champagne and lager proved to be a lethal cocktail. Somehow or other they piled into the team coach, cans of lager and all, and proceeded to Buckingham Palace where a tour of the picture gallery and state rooms had been arranged for them.

The Aussies more or less fell out of the bus and were then given the briefest possible tour, which finished up in the state ballroom, at one end of which stood the two great thrones, normally roped off but not so on this occasion.

The temptation was too much for Rodney Marsh who was by now beginning to struggle and feeling very weary. Searching for somewhere to rest he slumped down across one of the thrones and, turning to a member of the royal household, said, "Gee, princess, I don't know about you but I'm completely buggered."

Dennis Lillee, his friend, came to the rescue, dragged him off the throne and directed him towards some tea and cake to help him back to the world of the living.

*

The legacy of the rain, which had helped create such a wonderful waterslide the night before, was that it delayed Sussex's inevitable and anticlimactic victory on the final day of the season. It also gave everyone the chance to discuss the team streak which, by all accounts, had been much enjoyed by those few spectators who still happened to be at the ground and by the inhabitants of the flats overlooking.

"Surprisingly, perhaps, we have received no complaints," said a club official.

Roy Stevens, the Sussex chief executive, was less committal in his response. "I did not see the incident, but we are looking into the matter." I don't think anyone ever bothered.

When play did finally get under way, it took until after lunch to separate the partnership between Hartley and Hampshire despite some exceptionally hostile fast bowling from Imran and le Roux, who was actually warned by Pakistan's visiting umpire, Mahboob Shah, for bowling a series of bouncers in one over.

There was no letting up in our final thrust for victory.

In mid-afternoon Bairstow arrived at the crease and suggested in a most innocent way that, if le Roux pitched the ball up and straight, he would obligingly miss one and so hasten an end to proceedings. Le Roux fell for this old trick, hook, line and sinker, and Bairstow thumped a succession of gentle half-volleys back past him for four. Le Roux was outraged that Bairstow had failed to keep his side of the bargain when in truth he had been fooled, in the dying moments of the season, by some cunning gamesmanship.

For all this bravado Yorkshire did not last long and, when we came to tackle a modest victory target of 102, they were more intent upon improving their over rate and avoiding a fine than preventing us from reaching our final goal. There was a sense of unreality about the cricket as the curtain came down upon the season.

Jim Love, not known hitherto for his bowling skills, was tossing up some very occasional off-spinners to me from two paces when he performed a remarkable feat, the like of which I had never seen before. He bowled a very slow, flighty ball outside my off-stump which, as I drove at it, spun sharply back at me and so slow was it that I had time to turn and watch the ball neatly bisect my off and middle stumps without dislodging a bail. Behind the wicket Bairstow stared, open-mouthed and lost for words. It was as if the stumps had parted and come back together again by way of a cricketing conjuring trick. With only a few more runs left to score, it was rather a waste of some extraordinarily good luck.

Moments later the match was won.

CHAMPIONSHIP TABLE – 15 SEPTEMBER

		Played	Points
1.	Nottinghamshire	22	304
2.	Sussex	22	302
3.	Somerset	22	279
4.	Middlesex	22	257

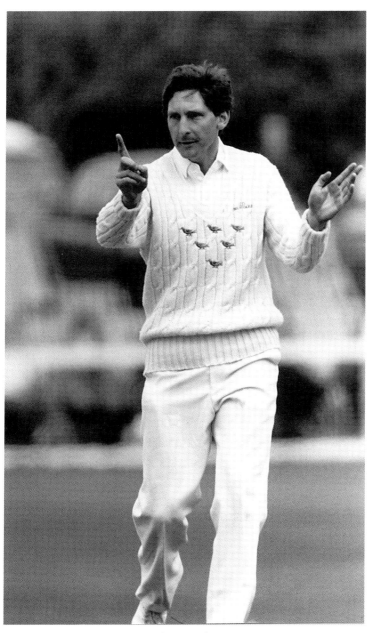

John Barclay

Chapter Sixteen

A Summer to Remember

This has been the story of the 1981 season and how it unfolded and how, in my first summer as captain of Sussex, I sought to lead the county to its first ever championship victory. We came agonisingly close, but in the end failed by just two points.

My immediate reaction was not one of disappointment but rather of elation. We had aspired to great things and had played a lot of wonderful cricket along the way. Anyone who took part in, or who watched, the games at Tunbridge Wells and Trent Bridge, at Leicester and Eastbourne, will have enjoyed county cricket at its very best.

We won eleven matches, and none of those wins came from opposition declarations. Each time we bowled our opponents out twice.

It had been an exhilarating summer, each match some sort of frantic drama, played at a blistering pace.

"You must all be on pills," the umpire Bill Alley remarked about half way through the season. "You can't play like this all the time."

Yes, we were headstrong, the adrenalin was pumping and we were tasting success.

The county championship is the true Grand National of cricket. It is a complete examination of skills and techniques, run over a course that takes in widely varying conditions and surfaces, and littered with testing obstacles, where the unexpected is never far away. It stretches every nerve and sinew of the body and brain and, above all else, is a great test of stamina.

We crept up fast and confident on the inside rail, but in the end Notts just held on.

The spirit of the Avisford Park get-together had carried on throughout the whole summer. We looked after one another in many ways, and that was most gratifying. Richard Streeton spotted this and wrote in *The Times*: 'There has been an unselfish and generous team spirit in the Sussex dressing room, which has not always been the case in recent years.'

I can't recall our ever losing that strength of spirit and desire to win. Even when we collapsed at Guildford or embarked upon that unsuccessful run chase against Kent, we still held our heads up high.

It is only with the passing of time that the disappointment of not winning the prize has grown. I can never quite put it to the back of my mind.

The 'what ifs' loom large.

What if the rain had not fallen so persistantly at Bristol and Lord's?

What if I had not overstepped the crease at Trent Bridge and so dismissed Hassan with my first ball of the second day?

What if Arnold had hit that last ball at Leicester for four? Or Peter Stevens had raised his finger and upheld the appeal against Mike Bore?

But such an exercise doesn't really help. Over the course of the season, we had also had our fair share of good luck. Satisfaction must be taken from what had been done, and not in what might have been.

And Notts played some fine cricket too. Rice had relied mainly upon his pace bowling along with that of Hadlee and supported admirably by the spin of Hemmings. All three of them had bowled magnificently. It is true that wickets were prepared to help them, but then we did just the same at Eastbourne. Championship cricket is all the better for games which encourage positive results.

*

Our strong team spirit may indeed have emanated in part from my own shortcomings as a player. I have noticed that most cricketers reach the position of captain having themselves excelled with bat or ball or both. That was not the case for me.

I found that not being the best player in the side was actually an advantage. Like Mike Brearley, who captained England and Middlesex in a similar way, rather less was expected of me as a player. When I was out for nought, heads hardly slumped

Of course I would love to have been a brilliant player, but I wasn't and so I tried to use my average abilities to my advantage as captain. The great players who come to captaincy are sometimes tempted to tell or show their players how to play. That can be counter-productive and often doesn't work. I believe cricketers do better when they reach conclusions for themselves. I wanted us to become a thinking team.

For example, I would frequently throw ideas around the slip cordon and flick out suggestions asking each player in turn what they thought. Parker from cover point was always full of ideas. It was fun and inspiring and kept the opposition guessing too.

Imran and I would stay in contact from a longer distance as he didn't like fielding close to the wicket. I used to say to him, "Think about when you would like to bowl," and I would just wait for his signal. And, as at Eastbourne, his instinct was often right.

By doing this I felt I was bringing the team into the decision-making process, although Gould has often told me he saw it quite differently.

"Basically," he said, "you always knew what you wanted to do but just waited until the actual suggestion came from someone else."

But everyone playing cricket has thoughts, and as captain I was the channel through which these could be put into practice. When players came up with an idea I felt I owed it to them to give it a go. If it was tried for two or three overs and didn't work, at least it had been given a whirl. And if it did come off much pleasure was the result. Players grew in confidence when they felt they were part of the decision making. Although I had a gentle exterior, I think there was some steel in me, and I was also very competitive. I was fascinated by different methods of leadership and finding ways to win.

*

We had finished the summer on a note of unbridled optimism. Our abiding feeling was that we would win the championship the next year. And, indeed, we did start 1982 as we had left off in 1981. By late June we were near the top of both the championship and Sunday League tables and also through to the semi-finals of the Benson and Hedges Cup for the first time.

At which point Imran left us to captain Pakistan, and Greig was called up to play two Test matches for England. Our potency was reduced. We did however win the Sunday League title but lost momentum in the championship. Arnold retired, Imran and le Roux were both injured in 1983 and, though our ambition to win never dwindled, the feeling that we could take on and beat anybody did diminish somewhat.

But cricket is all about people, not just trophies, and that team of 1981 became a part of my life. It was a very happy chapter in the history of Sussex cricket, a summer to remember, and the friendships have endured well beyond our cricket-playing days.

Sussex will win the championship some day. It is a four-day game now, with two divisions, but the essence of the competition remains the same and, when the time comes, the joy will be very great.

Then there will be another story to tell, quite a different one, and filled with new characters and fresh emotion. I shall enjoy reading it.

FINAL COUNTY CHAMPIONSHIP TABLE

		Played	Won	Lost	Drawn	NR	Bonus Points Batting	Bowling	Points
1	Nottinghamshire	22	11	4	6	1	56	72	304
2	Sussex	22	11	3	6	2	58	68	302
3	Somerset	22	10	2	10	0	54	65	279
4	Middlesex	22	9	3	9	1	49	64	257
5	Essex	22	8	4	9	1	62	64	254
6	Surrey	22	7	5	9	1	52	72	236
7	Hampshire	22	6	7	8	1	45	65	206
8	Leicestershire	22	6	6	9	1	45	58	199
9	Kent	22	5	7	10	0	51	58	189
10	Yorkshire	22	5	9	8	0	41	66	187
11	Worcestershire	22	5	9	8	0	44	52	172
12	Derbyshire	22	4	7	10	1	51	57	172
13	Gloucestershire	22	4	3	12	3	51	55	170
14	Glamorgan	22	3	10	8	1	50	69	167
15	Northamptonshire	22	3	6	12	1	51	67	166
16	Lancashire	22	4	7	11	0	47	57	164
17	Warwickshire	22	2	11	9	0	56	47	135

CHAMPIONSHIP AVERAGES

BATTING

	M	I	NO	HS	Runs	Average	100s
P.W.G. Parker	18	32	9	136	1263	54.91	4
G.D. Mendis	20	36	3	137	1420	43.03	2
Imran Khan	18	27	6	107*	857	40.80	2
C.M. Wells	10	16	4	111	375	31.25	1
I.A. Greig	20	30	4	118*	789	30.34	1
J.R.T. Barclay	20	34	3	107*	865	27.90	2
I.J. Gould	20	25	3	52	594	27.00	-
G.S. le Roux	19	20	7	65*	340	26.15	-
C.P. Phillipson	18	25	9	56*	379	23.68	-
T.D. Booth-Jones	14	24	0	95	509	21.20	-
G.G. Arnold	18	17	7	46*	180	18.00	-
C.E. Waller	20	13	5	22	76	9.50	-

Played in two matches: J.R.P. Heath 9, 14*, 28   A.N. Jones 4
Played in one match: A.C.S. Pigott did not bat

BOWLING

	Overs	Maidens	Runs	Wickets	Best	Average
G.S. le Roux	559.1	133	1582	81	8-107	19.53
I.A. Greig	400.5	82	1264	60	6-21	21.06
Imran Khan	565.1	137	1464	66	6-52	22.18
G.G. Arnold	458.1	122	1121	40	6-39	28.02
J.R.T. Barclay	337.5	82	839	28	4-47	29.96
C.E. Waller	435.1	118	1137	37	5-36	30.72

A.N. Jones   19-3-63-4   C.M. Wells   19-4-56-2
A.C.S. Pigott   14-2-39-2   P.W.G. Parker   3-3-0-0
I.J. Gould   3-1-2-0

FIELDING

61   I.J. Gould (57 ct, 4 st)
28   J.R.T. Barclay
26   C.P. Phillipson
14   P.W.G. Parker
12   I.A. Greig
11   C.E. Waller

7   G.G. Arnold
6   Imran Khan, G.S. le Roux,
        G.D. Mendis
5   T.D. Booth-Jones
2   C.M. Wells
1   J.R.P. Heath, A.C.S. Pigott

SUMMARY OF SUSSEX CRICKET IN 1981

COUNTY CHAMPIONSHIP RESULTS

At Worcester. May 6,7,8
Sussex (3 pts) drew with Worcestershire (4 pts)
Sussex   252 for 8 dec
                  163 for 2 dec (Mendis 79*, Barclay 55)
Worcestershire   158 for 0 dec (Turner 104*)
                  145 for 4

At Hove. May 13,14,15
Sussex (21 pts) beat Glamorgan (6 pts) by 7 wickets
Glamorgan   230   (Jones 109)
              119   (Arnold 6-39)
Sussex   195
              155 for 3

At Lord's. May 23,25,26
Middlesex v Sussex
Match abandoned

At Bristol. May 27,28,29
Gloucestershire v Sussex
Match abandoned

At Hove. June 3,4,5
Sussex (6 pts) drew with Somerset (4 pts)
Sussex   360 for 6 dec (Booth-Jones 95, Parker 108, Imran 74)
              164 for 8 dec
Somerset   272 for 9 dec (Denning 72, Garner 52)
              152 for 5

At Hove. June 6,8,9
Sussex (24 pts) beat Lancashire (2 pts) by an innings and 62 runs
Sussex   397 for 7 dec (Parker 136, Greig 71, Phillipson 56*)
Lancashire   131
              204   (Greig 6-21)

At Tunbridge Wells. June 13,15,16
Kent (20 pts) beat Sussex (7 pts) by 37 runs
Kent   250 for 8 dec   (Asif 76, Knott 52)
                        270 for 5 dec   (Taylor 99, Tavare 88)
Sussex   301 for 5 dec   (Barclay 65, Mendis 55,
                                             Booth-Jones 60, Parker 60*)
                        182   (Mendis 80, Jarvis 5-82)

At Northampton. June 17,18,19
Northamptonshire (7 pts) drew with Sussex (3 pts)
Northamptonshire 300 for 2 dec   (Cook 146*, Williams 133)
                        252 for 6 dec   (Lamb 102*)
Sussex   250 for 7 dec   (Barclay 107*)
                        111 for 3   (Parker 53*)

At Ilford. June 20,22,23
Sussex (24 pts) beat Essex (2 pts) by an innings and 21 runs
Sussex   436 for 4 dec   (Mendis 119, Parker 132, Imran 98*)
Essex   169
                        246   (Lilley 61)

At Hove. July 4,6,7
Sussex (7 pts) drew with Gloucestershire (6 pts)
Sussex   304   (Mendis 78)
                        197 for 3 dec   (Mendis 95, Parker 50*)
Gloucestershire   285   (Zaheer 145, Waller 5-94)
                        159 for 8   (Stovold 57)

At Taunton. July 11,13,14
Sussex (22 pts) beat Somerset (4 pts) by 6 wickets
Somerset   104
                        367   (Rose 82, Lloyds 68, Denning 61,
                                             Botham 72, le Roux 8-107)
Sussex   233   (le Roux 65*, Botham 6-90)
                        242 for 4   (Booth-Jones 75, Parker 105*)

At Hove. July 15,16,17
Sussex (6 pts) drew with Surrey (4 pts)

Surrey	175	(Knight 61)
	90 for 3	
Sussex	289	(Parker 58, Greig 78*, Gould 52, Intikhab 5-44)

At Hove. July 18,20,21
Sussex (22 pts) beat Warwickshire (6 pts) by 5 wickets

Warwickshire	249	(Lloyd 89, Asif Din 57)
	126	(Amiss 58, le Roux 6-36)
Sussex	208	
	169 for 5	(Parker 50)

At Guildford. July 29,30,31
Surrey (23 pts) beat Sussex (8 pts) by 5 wickets

Sussex	302	(Imran 92)
	127	(Thomas (5-31)
Surrey	311	(Clinton 60, Lynch 75)
	119 for 5	

At Leicester. August 1,3,4
Leicestershire (22 pts) beat Sussex (4 pts) by 3 runs

Leicestershire	358 for 8 dec	(Steele 97, Briers 116, le Roux 5-83)
	155 for 3 dec	(Steele 51)
Sussex	250 for 7 dec	(Barclay 101)
	260	(Mendis 137, Cook 7-81)

At Eastbourne. August 8,10,11
Sussex (24 pts) beat Kent (4 pts) by 8 wickets

Sussex	310 for 9 dec	(Mendis 61, Barclay 79, Greig 86, Jarvis 6-66)
	51 for 2	
Kent	104	
	254	(Tavaré 72, Cowdrey 97)

At Eastbourne. August 12,13,14
Sussex (23 pts) beat Derbyshire (6 pts) by 5 wickets

Derbyshire	256	(Wright 73, Kirsten 85)
	227	(Kirsten 68, Steele 59, Imran 5-52)
Sussex	250 for 7 dec	(Parker 82*)
	235 for 5	(Imran 107*)

At Trent Bridge. August 15,17,18
Nottinghamshire (4 pts) drew with Sussex (6 pts)
Sussex	208	(Mendis 65, Hemmings 5-94)
	144	
Nottinghamshire	102	(Hassan 58*, Waller 5-36)
	223 for 9	(Hassan 79, Rice 58)

At Bournemouth. August 26,27,28
Sussex (22 pts) beat Hampshire (4 pts) by 8 wickets
Hampshire	148	
	223	(Turner 64)
Sussex	237	(Imran 100, Marshall 6-62)
	135 for 2	(Mendis 51)

At Hove. August 29,31, September 1
Sussex (23 pts) beat Middlesex (5 pts) by 10 wickets
Middlesex	154	
	157	(Radley 51, Imran 6-52)
Sussex	252	(Gould 51, Hughes 5-94)
	60 for 0	

At Hove. September 2,3,4
Sussex (24 pts) beat Hampshire (5 pts) by 9 wickets
Sussex	416 for 7 dec	(Mendis 58, Wells 111, Greig 118*)
	24 for 1	
Hampshire	241	(Rice 101*, Greig 6-75)
	196	

At Hove. September 12,14,15
Sussex (23 pts) beat Yorkshire (3 pts) by 8 wickets
Yorkshire	153	
	198	(Hampshire 53)
Sussex	250 for 5 dec	(Wells 80)
	102 for 2	

OTHER FIRST-CLASS MATCHES

At Fenner's. June 10,11,12
Sussex beat Cambridge University by an innings and 40 runs

Sussex	348 for 9 dec	(C. Wells 79, Greig 50, A. Wells 63, Waller 51*)
Cambridge U	165	(Holliday 57, Greig 5-45)
	143	(Greig 7-43)

At Hastings. June 27,29,30
Sussex beat Sri Lankans by 82 runs

Sussex	161	
	228 for 6 dec	(Heath 101*)
Sri Lankans	158	(Devapriya 56)
	149	(Hettiaratchy 57)

At Hove. August 22,23,24
Australians beat Sussex by 7 wickets

Sussex	150	(Whitney 5-60)
	261	(Heath 56, Head 52*)
Australians	236	(Hughes 52)
	176 for 3	(Dyson 65*, Hughes 70*)

LIMITED OVER CRICKET

NATWEST BANK TROPHY
Knocked out in Quarter-Finals

Edgbaston. July 22,23	Beat Warwickshire by 124 runs
Hove. August 5 (Q-F)	Lost to Essex by 25 runs

BENSON AND HEDGES CUP
Knocked out in Quarter-Finals.

Hove. May 11	Beat Surrey by 3 wickets
Lord's. May 19,20	No result v Middlesex
Slough. May 21, 22	Beat Minor Counties by 46 runs
Hove. May 30, June 1	Beat Hampshire by 3 wickets
Hove. June 24,25 (Q-F)	Lost to Leicestershire by 4 wickets

JOHN PLAYER SUNDAY LEAGUE

Fifth Place in Table	**Won 8, Lost 5, No Result 3**
Hove. May 10	No result v Surrey
Worcester. May 17	Beat Worcestershire by 8 wickets
Lord's. May 24	No result v Middlesex
Basingstoke. May 31	Beat Hampshire by 7 wickets
Hove. June 7	Beat Lancashire on faster scoring rate
Ilford. June 21	Beat Essex by 3 wickets
Hastings. June 28	Lost to Northamptonshire by 5 runs
Hove. July 5	Beat Gloucestershire by 51 runs
Taunton. July 12	Lost to Somerset by 4 wickets
Horsham. July 19	Lost to Warwickshire by 7 wickets
Ebbw Vale. July 26	Beat Glamorgan by 88 runs
Leicester. August 2	Beat Leicestershire by 3 wickets
Eastbourne. August 9	Lost to Kent on faster scoring rate
Trent Bridge. August 16	Lost to Nottinghamshire by 4 wickets
Hove. September 6	Beat Derbyshire by 5 wickets
Hove. September 13	No result v Yorkshire

INDEX

The following appear throughout:

Geoff Arnold, John Barclay, Tim Booth-Jones, Ian Gould, Ian Greig, Imran Khan, Garth le Roux, Gehan Mendis, Paul Parker, Paul Phillipson, Chris Waller, Colin Wells